ISBN 978-1-333-87180-2
PIBN 10277207

This book is a reproduction of an important historical work. Forgotten Books uses
state-of-the-art technology to digitally reconstruct the work, preserving the original format
whilst repairing imperfections present in the aged copy. In rare cases, an imperfection in
the original, such as a blemish or missing page, may be replicated in our edition. We do,
however, repair the vast majority of imperfections successfully; any imperfections that
remain are intentionally left to preserve the state of such historical works.

1 MONTH OF
FREE
READING

at

www.ForgottenBooks.com

By purchasing this book you are
eligible for one month membership to
ForgottenBooks.com, giving you
unlimited access to our entire
collection of over 1,000,000 titles via
our web site and mobile apps.

To claim your free month visit:

www.forgottenbooks.com/free277207

English
Français
Deutsche
Italiano
Español
Português

www.forgottenbooks.com

Mythology Photography **Fiction**
Fishing Christianity **Art** Cooking
Essays Buddhism Freemasonry
Medicine **Biology** Music **Ancient
Egypt** Evolution Carpentry Physics
Dance Geology **Mathematics** Fitness
Shakespeare **Folklore** Yoga Marketing
Confidence Immortality Biographies
Poetry **Psychology** Witchcraft
Electronics Chemistry History **Law**
Accounting **Philosophy** Anthropology
Alchemy Drama Quantum Mechanics
Atheism Sexual Health **Ancient History**
Entrepreneurship Languages Sport
Paleontology Needlework Islam
Metaphysics Investment Archaeology
Parenting Statistics Criminology
Motivational

GENEALOGICAL SKETCHES

ALLEN FAMILY

OF MEDFIELD,

WITH AN ACCOUNT OF THE CELEBRATION OF THE
GOLDEN WEDDING OF ELLIS AND LUCY ALLEN,

with the Address read at the same:

ALSO AN ACCOUNT OF THE GOLDEN WEDDING OF
GERSHOM AND ABIGAIL [ALLEN] ADAMS,

BY THEIR ELDER BROTHER,

JOSEPH ALLEN,

OF NORTHBOROUGH.

BOSTON:
NICHOLS AND NOYES,

GENEALOGICAL SKETCHES

OF THE

ALLEN FAMILY

OF MEDFIELD;

WITH AN ACCOUNT OF THE CELEBRATION OF THE
GOLDEN WEDDING OF ELLIS AND LUCY ALLEN,

With the Address read at the Same.

ALSO AN ACCOUNT OF THE GOLDEN WEDDING OF
GERSHOM AND ABIGAIL [ALLEN] ADAMS.

BY THEIR ELDER BROTHER,

JOSEPH ALLEN,

OF NORTHBOROUGH.

BOSTON:
NICHOLS AND NOYES,
117, WASHINGTON STREET.
1869.

INTRODUCTION.

THE following tables are termed " Sketches," as they do not pretend to give a complete genealogy of the family of which JAMES ALLEN was the progenitor. Thus, of the nine children of James, I have taken only one, JOSEPH, the youngest son of JAMES. And of the ten sons and two daughters of Joseph, I have attempted to trace the line of descent only through five of his sons. And, though I have sought information through such sources as were accessible, I have not been able to obtain complete and satisfactory answers relating to those five.

The work, imperfect as it is, has cost me not a little labor. Yet that labor has not been a task, but a pastime; occupying some of my leisure hours, at an age when we live more in the past than in the future, or even in the present. I now commend it to the favor of the prolific family that can trace their descent from their common progenitor, JAMES ALLEN, of Medfield.

NOTE. — The Roman letters indicate the generation; JAMES being the first [I.], JOSEPH the second [II.], &c.

The numbers 1, 2, 3, 4, &c., indicate the members of one entire family, or the children of the same parents.

The descendants of each of the five sons of Joseph are grouped together, so that the line of descent can be traced from each, independent of the others.

GENEALOGY.

JAMES ALLEN, the progenitor of the Allen Family of Medfield, came over, with his wife Anna, in 1639 [freeman in 1647], and settled in Dedham; of which town his cousin, John Allin, was the first minister. Here he lived about ten years; and here, Dec. 4, 1639, his eldest son, John, was born.

James was one of a company formed, in 1649, to found a settlement in the western part of Dedham, bordering on Charles River, which, the following year, was incorporated by the name of "Medfield." The company consisted of fifty persons, each of whom was to have a house-lot of not more than twelve acres of upland, and as many of meadow. Other grants were subsequently made, which, together with purchases from time to time, constituted the Allen farm, which has remained in the family more than two hundred years, and is now in the possession of descendants of James, of the sixth and seventh generation.

That James was a relative of Rev. John Allin, appears from the following clause in the last will and testament of the latter: "I give and bequeath to my *cousin* James Allin, of Medfield, twenty shillings," &c. The will was made Aug. 23, 1671, three days before his death, which took place Aug. 26, 1671, at the age of seventy-five.

NOTE. — Rev. JOHN ALLIN was born in 1596; came over and settled in Dedham in 1637, of which town he became the pastor in 1639.
"He had," says Cotton Mather, "an easy sickness of ten days. His
beloved wife Katherine died three days after, and they were both
buried in the same grave." She was his second wife, the widow of
Governor Thomas Dudley, and was married to Rev. John Allin,
Nov. 8, 1653, only three months after the death of Governor Dudley,
and a little more than six months after the death of Margaret his
first wife. By his second wife, he had three sons, — Benjamin, Daniel,
and Eliezer. Rev. John Allen was from Wrentham, Suffolk County,
England, which name was given to a part of Dedham.

In the old records, the name is spelled variously, — Allen, Allin,
and Alin.

    I. **James,** by his wife Anna, had nine children : —

        1. JOHN, b. in Dedham, Dec. 4, 1639.

        2. JAMES, b. in Medfield; m. Lydia Adams.

        3. NATHANIEL, m. Mary Frizwell in 1673; had nine
children, viz., Samuel, Nathaniel, James, John,
Mary, Ann, Ebenezer, Sarah Benjamin, and
Edward.

        4. WILLIAM, who had Mary and William, besides
two who died in infancy.

        5. BENJAMIN, who had Benjamin, Mary, and Lydia.

        6. MARTHA, m. William Sabine, of Seekonk, R.I.,
Dec. 22, 1663.

        7. MARY, m. Joseph Clark, of Medfield.

        8. SARAH, m. Domingo White, in 1666.

        9. **Joseph,** b. June 24, 1652; m. Hannah Sabine, of
Seekonk.

    II. **Joseph,** by his wife Hannah, had twelve chil-
        dren ; viz. : —

        1. JOSEPH, b. Dec. 19, 1676.

        2. HANNAH, b. 1679.

        3. DANIEL, b. 1681; } removed to Pomfret, Conn.
        4. DAVID, b. 1683; }

        5. NOAH, b. April 21, 1685; m. Sarah Gay, of Ded-
ham.

6. 𝕰𝖑𝖎𝖊𝖟𝖊𝖗, b. 1688 ; m. Mary Battelle, of Dover.
7. JEREMIAH, b. 1690; not married.
8. 𝕳𝖊𝖟𝖊𝖐𝖎𝖆𝖍, b. 1692.
9. ABIGAIL, b. 1694.
10. 𝕹𝖊𝖍𝖊𝖒𝖎𝖆𝖍, bap. May 21, 1699.
11 and 12. THANKFUL and MARY.

Of these twelve children of Joseph and Hannah Allen, I have been able to obtain reliable information of only four, — Noah, Eliezer, Hezekiah, and Nehemiah, — with a brief account of Joseph, the eldest son.

III. JOSEPH ALLEN, Jr., married, Nov. 4, 1701, Miriam Wight, of Medfield, by whom he had —

1. JOSEPH, 3d, bap. Aug. 16, 1702.
2. MIRIAM, bap. May 27, 1704 ; d. March 3, 1727–8.
3. MOSES, bap. Sept. 20, 1708.
4. AARON, bap. March 11, 1715–6.

The above-named sons of Joseph Allen, Jr., — viz., Joseph Allen, 3d, Moses, and Aaron, — about the year 1736 removed, with their uncle Nehemiah, to Sturbridge; two of whom, Joseph and Moses, were town-officers the year following the incorporation of that town, 1738.

Another of the progenitors of the Allens of Sturbridge was Isaac Allen, also from Medfield.

IV. Joseph Allen, 3d, before his removal to Sturbridge, married, Dec. 18, 1727, Sarah Parker, to whom were born, in Medfield, two sons and one daughter.

1. ASA, b. Feb. 18, 1729.
2. OLIVE, b. April 2, 1732.
3. JOSEPH, b. July 6, 1734.

NOTE. — The following instrument, found among the old papers that have been preserved, shows that one of the sons of Joseph Allen, Sr., viz., Daniel, lived in Pomfret, near Woodstock, Conn. : —

"Know all men by these presents, that I, Daniel Allen, of Pomfret, in the County of Windham, Conn., having received of my brother Noah Allen, of Medfield, the sum of six pounds in bills of credit, upon which account I do acquit and discharge the estate of my honored father Joseph Allen, and the estate of my brother Jeremiah

Allen; having received my full share, to my content and satisfaction. I do discharge my brother Noah Allen, his heirs and assigns, from any further legacy to pay to me upon the above said account; whereto I have set my hand and seal, this second day of June, 1735.   (Signed)   DANIEL ALLEN."

From another old document, it appears, that, in 1731, Joseph Lawrence, of Pomfret, and his wife Mary [probably a sister of Daniel], sold a parcel of land in Medfield, near "Warren Lot," to Noah Allen, which remained for many years a part of the Allen estate.

It appears, moreover, that Joseph Allen, Sr., gave to his two sons, Daniel and David, a hundred acres of land in a place called "Massamoquit, near Woodstock, Conn., where they settled, and probably had families, who extended the name in that neighborhood. I learn, from Ezra Dean, Esq., of Woodstock, who married a granddaughter of Jacob Allen, Jr., that David Allen lived in Ashford, Conn., whose sons — Solomon, David, and Zechariah — died many years since. Mr. Dean's grandmother, Jemima, was a sister of this David Allen. They died some sixty years since.

III. **Noah,** the fourth son of Joseph Allen, Sr., by his wife Sarah [Gay] Allen, had seven children : —

1. SARAH, b. 1714; m. Joshua Boyden, of Medfield.
2. THANKFUL, b. 1718; m. Seth Clark, of Medfield.
3. NOAH, bap. Nov. 8, 1719; m. Miriam Fisher.
4. JEREMIAH, bap. Oct. 8, 1720; unmarried.
5. ELIJAH, bap. Feb. 3, 1723; m. Sarah Morse.
6. SYBIL, bap. Dec. 20, 1724; m. Sylvanus Plimpton.
7. JONATHAN, bap. Oct. 30, 1726; m. Sarah, d. of Samuel Ellis.

IV. **Sarah** had three children, — CATY, ASA, and a daughter, name unknown.
Thankful had one child, EBENEZER.
Elijah had five children; viz. : — '

1. SARAH, b. June 7, 1755; m. Philip Blake, of Wrentham.
2. SYBIL, b. April 7, 1757; m. Rufus Mann, Medfield.

3. CATHERINE, b. Feb. 14, 1759 ; m. Oliver Hartshorn, Medfield.
4. THANKFUL, b. Feb. 25, 1761 ; m. John Bullard,
   Medfield.
5. ABIGAIL, b. Oct. 12, 1771 ; m. Noah Daniels,
   Medfield.

V. Children of SARAH [ALLEN] BLAKE : —:
1. PATTY, b. July 2, 1780 ; m. Eli Messenger ; d.
   1824.
2. JOSIAH, b. April 16, 1782 ; m. Mary Barbour ;
   d. Aug. 4, 1858.
3. ALLEN, b. Sept. 4, 1784 ; d. Sept. 24, 1804.
4. SARAH, b. Oct. 25, 1786 ; m. Henry Campbell ;
   d. 1811.
5. HEPSIBETH, b. June 16, 1788 ; m. Asa Fuller.
6. IRA, b. Oct. 19, 1790 ; m. Laura Maury ; d. Sept.
   28, 1848.

Ira was the father of Rev. Mortimer Blake, D.D., of Taun-
ton, Mass.

V. Children of SYBIL [ALLEN] MANN : —
1. SARAH, m. Daniel Everett ; lived in Foxborough.
2. RODNEY, died in Buenos Ayres, S.A.
3. SUSAN, m. Timothy Whitney, and lived in Wrentham.
4. GEORGE, m. —— Fisher, of Medway, and lived
   in Dedham.
5. GERAULD NEWLON EZRA, m. Betsey Kingsbury,
   and lived in Dedham.

V. Children of CATHERINE [ALLEN] HARTSHORN : —
1. WILLIAM ; 2. JOHN ; 3. LUCINDA ; and 4. BRATON.

IV. SYBIL [ALLEN] PLYMPTON [daughter of Noah] had
   two children : —

V. 1. SARAH, m. *Master* Eleazer Wheelock, of Medfield.

   2. JONATHAN, lived first in Shrewsbury, afterwards in West Boylston. He had two sons; viz. : —

VI. 1. OLIVER, died in West Boylston.

   2. SIMON, removed to Holliston.

SYBIL, after the death of her first husband, married James Tisdale, of West Dedham.

IV. **Jonathan,** youngest son of Noah and Sarah Allen, had by his wife Sarah [Ellis] Allen —

   1. OLIVER, m. Sally Allen, of Walpole; d. in 1796.

   2. OLIVE, m. Aaron Clark, of Medfield.

   3. ABIGAIL, m. Phineas Partridge, of Franklin.

Oliver, by his wife Sally, had one child; viz., —

VI. WILLARD, m. Charlotte Hill, of Walpole, by whom he had five children : —

   1. WILLARD J.

   2. REUEL.

   3. SARAH ANN.

   4. OLIVER JOHNSON.

   5. ALBERT S.

Jonathan Allen lived on a farm contiguous to the old homestead: he was a cooper by trade, as had been his progenitors for several generations.

IV. **Noah Allen,** Jr., by his first wife, Miriam, had five sons : —

   1. ASAHEL, b. 1745; d. Jan. 24, 1784, age 40.

   2. FISHER, b. Feb. 6, 1747; d. June 21, 1842, age 95.

   3. SILAS, b. Nov. 20, 1749; d. April, 1834, age 85.

   4. NATHAN, b. June 1, 1753; d. April 10, 1848, age 95.

   5. GAD, bap. June 1, 1751; died in infancy.

   Miriam, the mother of these children, died June

23, 1757, leaving four children, all under twelve
years.

In 1761, March 12, Noah m. Abigail Ellis, by
whom he had two children : —

6. MIRIAM, b. 1762 ; m. Seth Kingsbury, of Walpole.
7. PHINEAS, b. April 24, 1764 ; d. Aug. 13, 1836,
aged 73.

The mother died July 28, 1764, when Phineas was only
three months old.

Noah m. for his third wife Sybil [Clark] Smith, widow
of Elisha Smith, and sister of Rev. Pitt Clark, of Norton.
By her first husband, she had two daughters, Olive and
Sybil. The elder m. James Holbrook ; the younger m. a
person by the name of Corson. Noah d. March 23, 1804,
aged 85.

Of the children of NOAH, —

Asahel lived in Medfield.

Fisher inherited the estate of his grandfather Fisher, for
whom he was named, and who lived in Dover.

Silas lived first in Medfield, and afterwards in Shrewsbury.

Nathan lived in Medfield.

Phineas lived with his father, and inherited the homestead.

V. **Asahel,** eldest son of Noah, m. Patience Richardson, of Medway. Their children were —

1. DAVID, b. July 26, 1776 ; d. Nov. 9, 1857, aged
81.
2. JEREMIAH, b. March 7, 1778 ; d. Feb. 14, 1862,
aged 84.
3. JONATHAN, b. April 1, 1780 ; d. June 5, 1815, —
drowned in Paris, Me.
4. PATIENCE, b. April 20, 1784. Still living, aged 85.

VI. **David,** m. Mary Fullum, lived in Leominster. They had seven children : —

1. ASAHEL, b. June 15, 1803 ; m. Nancy R. Kemson.
2. LOUISA, b. April 15, 1806 ; d. Nov. 15, 1832.
3. SARAH, b. Nov. 6, 1810 ; d. Nov. 8, 1828.
4. MARY F., b. Sept. 7, 1812 ; d. July 7, 1845.
5 and 6. DOROTHY and DAVID C., b. July 30, 1815.
7. ELIZABETH, b. Oct. 3, 1820 ; d. Nov. 10, 1843.

VI. **Jeremiah,** m. Mary Kingsbury, of Needham ; lived in West Newton. Their children were five in number : —

1. MARY, b. Jan. 2, 1806 ; m. Ralph Day, of Dover.
2. REBECCA, died in infancy.
3. MARTHA, d. at the age of 18.
4. MARIA, b. Dec. 22, 1814 ; m. Gilbert Davis, Westboro'.
5. AUGUSTUS, b. Jan. 30, 1817 ; m. Maria Davis, by whom he had three children, — Alfred, Hattie, and Emma.

His second wife was Almira K. Haven, by whom he has one child, Dora. ·

VI. **Jonathan,** third son of Asahel Allen ; m. April 30, 1806, Sarah Houghton, of Princeton, by whom he had five children.

1. SARAH, b. July 2, 1807 ; m. Isaac Farwell, of Waltham ; d. Nov. 21, 1867, aged 60.
2. OTIS, b. Sept. 12, 1808 ; m. Louisa Bixby, of Litchfield, N.H. ; lives in Lowell.
3. CAROLINE, b. Nov. 8, 1809 ; m. Jotham Stone, of Hubbardston.
4. ELIZABETH, died in infancy.
5. JONATHAN, b. Oct. 10, 1815 ; m. Albina Fuller ; d. Sept. 28, 1855.

The widow of Jonathan, Jr., lives in Lowell.
The widow of Jonathan, Sr., d. June 12, 1867, aged 85.

VI. 𝕻𝖆𝖙𝖎𝖊𝖓𝖈𝖊, only daughter of Asahel Allen; m. Calvin Joscelyn, of Leominster, Feb. 17, 1805.

Their children were —

1. CAROLINE, b. 1806; d. Sept. 4, 1823, aged 17.
2. MARTHA ALLEN, b. 1808; m. Elijah Sawyer, of Lancaster.
3. ELLIS K., b. 1810; m. Harriet Colman.
4. JOHN, b. 1814; m. Ellen M. Kenney.
5. WILLIAM ALLEN, b. 1816; m. Adeline Howe.
6. LORIN, b. 1817; m. Lucy Ann White.
7. ABIGAIL R., b. 1820; d. 1831.
8. ELIZABETH, b. 1822; m. William Lawrence, of Boston.

VII. 𝕬𝖘𝖆𝖍𝖊𝖑, eldest son of David, by his wife Nancy R., had eight children, six of whom died in infancy. The other two were —

1. SARAH E., b. May 15, 1833.
2. MARY A., b. Dec. 3, 1844.

VII. 𝕷𝖔𝖚𝖎𝖘𝖆, m. James Fisk; had two children, Sarah E. and Henry A.

VII. 𝕾𝖆𝖗𝖆𝖍, another daughter of David, died unmarried.

VII. 𝕸𝖆𝖗𝖞 𝕱., m. Cyrus Kinsman; had two children, George H. and Mary L. After her death, her sister Dorothy H. was married to Mr. Kinsman. Their children are Frank E. and Arthur M.

VII. 𝕯𝖆𝖛𝖎𝖉 𝕮., youngest child of David, m. Lucy W. Lyon, who died April 7, 1853. Their children were Charles Francis, George Albert, and Helen Elizabeth, of whom only one, George Albert, survives.

VII. 𝕺tis, son of Jonathan Allen, has three children;
viz.: —

VIII. 1. Sarah Jane, b. July 8, 1832; m. Edward A.
Hosmer, who d. July 18, 1855. She then m.
Coudan Winch, of Philadelphia, and d. April
27, 1865.

2. Thomas Otis, b. April 29, 1835; m. Charlotte
Augusta Peirce, of Lowell. Their children are
Edward A., Jane Louisa, and Otis.

3. Charles Herbert, b. April 15, 1848.

Thomas Otis Allen now lives in Jacksonville, Fla.

Otis Allen, Esq., lives in Lowell.

Children of Fisher Allen, son of Noah Allen, Jr.: —

V. Fisher Allen, by his wife Rachel [Smith] Allen,
had —

1. Miriam, b. Oct. 29, 1772; m. Daniel Kingsbury,
Walpole.

2. Abigail, b. Oct. 12, 1774; m. Nathaniel Fisk, of
Holliston.

3. Rachel, b. Sept. 20, 1779; m. Daniel Mann, of
Dover.

Grandchildren of Fisher Allen, by his daughter Miriam:

VI. Miriam was the mother of ten children: —

1. Fisher Allen, Esq., lived in Weymouth; d. in
1859.

2. Susan, m. Dea. Joel Capen, of Dorchester.

3. Rachel, m. Samuel Thomson, of Roxbury.

4. Adaline, m. Ellis Clapp, of Walpole.

5. Daniel, killed by falling from a wagon.

6. Almira, m. William Richardson, Esq., of Boston.

7. Miriam, died young.

8. Abigail, m. James Fuller, of Walpole.

9. Elizabeth, m. Mr. Fairfield, of Boston.

10. Joanna, m. John Capen, Esq., of Boston.

Grandchildren of FISHER ALLEN, by his daughter Abigail : —

VI. **Abigail,** by her husband Nathaniel Fisk, had four children : —:

1. NOAH ALLEN, b. Aug. 26, 1799 ; m. Anna, daughter of Dr. Elias Mann, of Medfield.
2. SALLY, b. Nov. 23, 1800.
3. JOSIAH F., b. Feb. 6, 1802; d. in 1829.
4. NATHANIEL, b. Dec. 28, 1803 ; killed, by falling from a wagon, April 30, 1857.

Grandchildren of FISHER ALLEN, by his daughter Rachel : —

VI. RACHEL, who m. Daniel Mann, had five children : —

1. LYDIA, m. Rufus Battelle.
2. RACHEL ALLEN, m. Dea. Ralph Battelle, of Dover.
3. BETSEY, m. Luther Richards, of Dedham.
4. LUCY MARIA, m. Calvin Richards, of Dover.
5. DANIEL FISHER, m. Sarah Jane Battelle, Providence, R.I.
Another child, died in infancy.

V. **Silas,** son of Noah Allen, Jr., m. Priscilla, daughter of Simon Plimpton, of Medfield, who was born Jan. 21, 1753. Their children were —

1. ELIZABETH CUNNINGHAM, b. Feb. 28, 1773; d. Sept. 23, 1863.
2. ASAHEL, b. Feb. 6, 1775; d. Oct. 13, 1866, in Berlin, Wis., aged 91.
3. SIMON, b. May 29, 1777; d. May 7, 1785.
4. NOAH, b. Aug. 23, 1780; d. Jan. 4, 1845, in Shrewsbury.
5. SILAS, b. July 12, 1785; d. March 6, 1868.

Grandchildren of SILAS ALLEN, by his daughter Elizabeth : —

VI. **Elizabeth**, m. to Ephraim Hapgood.   Their children were —

VII. 1. MARTHA, m. Benjamin Flagg, of Boylston.

2. SIMON ALLEN, d. in infancy.

3. LUCY, m. Washington Hill, of Spencer, who had two children, Martha H. and Ephraim.

Grandchildren of SILAS ALLEN, by his son Asahel : —

VI. **Asahel**, oldest son of Silas Allen, m. first Lucy Hemmenway, and for his second wife Mary J., daughter of Hollis Parker, all of Shrewsbury. Their children were —

VII. 1. ASAHEL PLIMPTON, b. May 17, 1806.

2. LUCY HEMMENWAY, b. Feb. 15, 1809 ; d. April 18, 1842.

3. DANIEL WALDO, b. May 17, 1811 ; m. Marietta E. Carter.

4. ELIZABETH WALDO ; b. Aug. 17, 1813.

The mother of these four, *Mary J. Allen*, died Feb. 28, 1862.

VII. **Asahel P.**, the oldest son of Asahel, m. R. B. Haven, of Boston ; removed, with his father, to Lancaster, N.H.   His children were —

1. FREDERICK M., b. in Boston, 1832 ; d. in 1850, aged 18.

2. EDWARD F., b. in Worcester, 1833 ; m. Fanny Wayland.

3. HELEN, b. in Lancaster, N.H., 1835 ; m. Daniel Swett, of Manchester, N.H.   Their children are Josephine and Eugene.

4. SARAH E., b. 1837.

5. MARY A., b. 1840.

6. WILLIAM H., b. 1842 ; d. Feb. 8, 1863.
7. GEORGE L., b. 1845.
8. EDITH M., b. 1847; d. March 18, 1863.
9. ABBY A., b. 1850.
10. ALICE L., b. 1853.

VII. **Daniel W.**, another son of Asahel by his first wife, Marietta, had three children : —
1. HENRY CLAY, b. March 5, 1848.
2. CELESTIA ELIZABETH, b. July 10, 1850.
3. MARY MARIA, b. Oct. 3, 1851.

After the death of his wife Marietta, he married, January, 1855, Lettice Boyle, by whom he had one child.

4. LUCY CATHERINE, b. Sept. 7, 1856.

VII. **Elizabeth Waldo**, youngest child of Asahel Allen; m. Rev. William Day, of Cleveland, O. Their children are Mary E., Lucy W., Ursula A., and Julia S.

VI. **Noah**, son of Silas Allen, m. Irene Hemmenway, and lived in Shrewsbury. Their children were —
1. Lucy H., b. Oct. 3, 1804 ; m. Uriah Bartlett, of Northboro'.
2. JONAS H., b. Jan. 4, 1807 ; m. Clarinda D. Howe.
3. ELMIRA H., b. July, 1811 ; m. J. B. Plimpton, Shrewsbury.
4. ASA H., b. Nov. 22, 1815 ; m. Catherine Black.

VII. **Lucy H.**, eldest child of Noah Allen, had one child. FREDERIC L., b. March 31, 1847.

VII. **Jonas H.** had two sons : —
1. CHARLES L., lives in Grafton.
2. JAMES H., lives in Shrewsbury.

VII. **Elmira H.**, daughter of Noah Allen, had three children : —

1. LUCY ANN, b. May 8, 1834.
2. ALBERT H., b. Dec. 27, 1836.
3. NOAH ALLEN, b. Sept. 11, 1841.

VII. **Asa H.**, youngest son of Noah Allen, had eight children : —

1. ELIJAH L., b. April 17, 1838 ; d. Aug. 2, 1861.
2. MARIA I. H., b. July 12, 1839.
3. CYRUS B., b. March 14, 1841.
4. SIMON B., b. Dec. 6, 1842.
5. MYRON H., b. May 4, 1845.
6. CATHERINE E., b. March 18, 1847.
7. MARY E., b. Jan. 9, 1850 ; d. Jan. 8, 1852.
8. JEREMIE E., b. Sept. 4, 1854.

VI. **Silas Allen, Jr.**, had three children : —

1. CYRUS BULLARD, b. Jan. 3, 1807 ; d. in Philadelphia, 1844.
2. ARNOLD LAMB, b. March 25, 1808 ; m. Caroline M. Sumner, grand-daughter of Rev. Dr. Sumner ; d. without issue.
3. SIMON HAPGOOD, b. Nov. 8, 1811 ; m. Abby Pratt, Shrewsbury. Their children died in infancy.

V. **Nathan,** son of Noah Allen, Jr., had three children : —

1. AMY, b. Feb. 10, 1780 ; m. Quincy Fisher.
2. OBED, b. July 8, 1782 ; m. Caroline Harding.
3. NATHAN, b. June 13, 1784 ; m. Catherine Fisher ; d. about 1840.

VI. **Amy,** besides five children who died in infancy, had one son and two daughters who lived to maturity ; viz. : —

1. WILLIAM Q., b. July 27, 1809.
2. AMY ALMIRA, b. Dec. 13, 1811 ; m. John Ellis ;
    d. 1860.
3. MIRIAM, b. Feb. 14, 1817 ; m. Henry Bruce.

VII. William Q. m. Mary L. Harding. Their children
    are —
1. MARY ELLEN, b. Dec. 24, 1841.
2. SARAH HARDING, b. Sept. 26, 1843.

VI. Col. Obed Allen, son of Nathan, had two
    children : —
1. CAROLINE, b. Dec. 14, 1806 ; m. John A. Newell,
    of Dover.
2. OBED, b. Nov. 6, 1808 ; m. Betsey Newell, of
    Dover.

    Col. Allen is a farmer, and lives in Medfield.

VI. Nathan Allen, Jr., had six children : —
1. CATHERINE HINSDALE, b. June 10, 1810.
2. FISHER, b. Nov. 17, 1812 ; d. Oct. 10, 1834.
3. MARY ANN, b. Sept. 8, 1816.
4. LOUISA ADELAIDE, b. June 6, 1819.
5. LUCY MARIA, b. June 7, 1824 ; d. Dec. 12, 1852.
6. ALFRED, b. Feb. 24, 1827.

    Nathan Allen lived in Dedham.

VII. Catherine H. m. William H. Spear, Esq., of Ply-
    mouth, who died, leaving one son, William F.,
    who m. Carrie Whiting.

VII. Mary Ann m. James Aldrich, M.D., of Fall
    River, who died childless.

    Louisa Adelaide was a teacher in Plymouth.

    None of the children of Nathan are supposed to
    be living at this time.

V. 𝔓𝔥𝔦𝔫𝔢𝔞𝔰 𝔄𝔩𝔩𝔢𝔫, youngest son of Noah Allen,
   b. April 24, 1764; m. *Ruth*, daughter of Asa
   Smith, of Walpole, b. Feb. 28, 1769.   Their
   children were —

1. ABIGAIL, b. Nov. 12, 1788; d. Feb. 22, 1796.
2. JOSEPH, b. Aug. 15, 1790; m. Lucy Clarke Ware,
   of Cambridge.
3. ELLIS, b. Sept. 10, 1792 ; m. Lucy Lane, of Scituate.
4. SILAS [WILLIA⅃ WINTHROP], b. Jan. 25, 1795.
5. ASA SᴍITH, b. June 21, 1797; m. Lydia Kingsbury, and Martha J. Camp.
6. ABIGAIL, b. Oct. 5, 1799 ; m. Gershom Adams.
7. PHINEAS, b. Oct. 15, 1801; m. Clarissa Fiske, of
   Medfield.
8. NOAH, b. April 22, 1807; m. Paulina S. Whiting, of Dover.

   Phineas, the father of these children, d. Aug. 13,
   1836, aged 72 years and 4 months.
   Ruth, the mother, d. July 25, 1832, aged 63.
   After the death of his first wife, Phineas married
   Miss Eliza Turner, of Boston.
   Phineas was a farmer, and lived on the old home-
   stead.

VI. 𝔍𝔬𝔰𝔢𝔭𝔥 m. Lucy Clarke, eldest daughter of Rev.
    Dr. Henry Ware, Sr., Feb. 3, 1818.   Their
    children were —

1. MARY WARE, b. March 7, 1819.
2. JOSEPH HENRY, b. Aug. 21, 1820.
3. THOᴍAS PRENTISS, b. July 7, 1822; d. Nov. 26,
   1868.
4. ELIZABETH WATERHOUSE, b. June 29, 1824.
5. LUCY CLARKE, b. Oct. 29, 182ὶ.
6. EDWARD AUGUSTUS HOLYOKE, b. Aug. 15, 1828.
7. WILLIAᴍ FRANCIS, b. Sept. 5, 1830.

Of the children of Joseph and Lucy C. [Ware] Allen, —

VII. 𝕸𝖆𝖗𝖞 𝖂𝖆𝖗𝖊 m., Sept. 1, 1840, Dr. J. J. Johnson, of Northboro'. Their children were —

1. HARRIET HALL, b. May 16, 1842.
2. SARAH ELIZABETH, b. June 2, 1844 ; d. May 16, 1847.
3. RICHARD LEWIS, b. July 6, 1847 ; d. Aug. 10, 1852.
4. MARY LOUISA, b. March 7, 1851 ; d. Sept. 22, 1854.
5. ROBERT LEWIS, b. Oct. 15, 1855 ; d. June 17, 1861.
6. HENRY WARE, b. Oct. 5, 1859 ; d. July 8, 1861.
7. ETHEL (adopted), b. Oct. 6, 1860 ; d. Sept. 6, 1865.

Dr. Johnson, with his wife and daughter, now occupy the old Manse in Northboro', built, in 1817, by Rev. J. Allen, who, with his daughter Elizabeth, are inmates of the family.

VII. 𝕵𝖔𝖘𝖊𝖕𝖍 𝕳𝖊𝖓𝖗𝖞 m., May 22, 1845, Anna Minot Weld, of Jamaica Plain. Their children were —

1. LUCY CLARKE, b. in Jamaica Plain, May 7, 1846.
2. MARGARET WELD, b. in Jamaica Plain, July 10, 1847 ; d. Aug. 17, 1861.
3. MARY WARE, b. in Washington, April 23, 1850.
4. RICHARD MINOT, b. in Bangor, March 20, 1853.
5. GARDNER WELD, b. in Bangor, Jan. 19, 1856.
6. RUSSELL CARPENTER, b. in Jamaica Plain, Jan. 27, 1859.

NOTE. — Joseph Henry graduated at Harvard College in 1840. Ordained in Jamaica Plain, Oct. 18, 1843 ; took charge of the Unitarian Church in Washington, D.C., Aug. 22, 1847 ; and in Bangor, Me., Oct. 24, 1850–1857. Lived in Northboro' from 1863 to 1866, when he removed to Cambridge.

VII. **Thomas Prentiss** m., Nov. 17, 1846, Sarah Alexander Lord, of Northfield. Their children were:

1. GERTRUDE EVERETT, b. Aug. 31, 1847; d. June 10, 1865.
2. OTIS EVERETT, b. June 17, 1850.
3. ANNIE WARE, b. June 14, 1852; d. March, 1854.
4. CAROLINE PUTNAM, b. March 18, d. Aug. 19, 1855.
5. HELEN WARE, b. [N. Bedford] April 16, 1858.

NOTE. — Thomas Prentiss graduated at Harvard College in 1842. Ordained at Sterling, Nov. 18, 1846. Took charge of a Classical School in New Bedford in 1855; was Associate Principal of West Newton English and Classical School from 1864 to 1868; established an independent Family School in the summer of 1868; died the 26th of the November following, aged 46.

The eldest daughter, Gertrude, went to Charleston, S.C., in the spring of 1865, as a teacher, where she died June 10 of the same year.

VII. **Elizabeth Waterhouse** lives at the homestead in Northboro'.

VII. **Lucy Clarke** m., Oct. 1, 1857, Albert E. Powers, of Lansingburgh, N.Y.

They have one child, Joseph Allen Powers, born June 28, 1858; and an adopted daughter, Mabel Powers.

VII. **Edward A. H.** m., Sept. 5, 1855, Eugenia Sophia, daughter of Dr. Teulon, of Newton Corner. Their children are —

1. KENNETH, b. April 6, 1857.
2. HENRY WARE, b. July 6, 1861.
3. MARGARET ELIZABETH, b. June 17, 1863.
4. CAROLINE STETSON, b. February, 1865.
5. ALBERT PRENTISS, b. June 27, 1868.

NOTE. — Edward A. H. Allen is a graduate of Bridgewater Normal School; was a graduate and a professor of the Rensselaer Institute, Troy, N.Y.; and Principal of "Friends' Academy," New Bedford, from 1855 to 1869.

VII. **William Francis** m., July 2, 1862, Mary Tileston, daughter of Rev. Henry Lambert, of West Newton, who died March 23, 1865, leaving an infant, Katherine, b. Feb. 17, 1865; — m. again, June 30, 1868, Margaret Loring, daughter of John Andrews, Esq., of Newburyport.

NOTE. — William Francis graduated at Harvard College in 1851; was private teacher in the family of Mrs. Waller, New York, three years; spent two years in Europe; was Associate Principal of the West Newton English and Classical School from 1856 to 1863; was for two years in the employ of the Freedmen's Aid and Western Sanitary Commissions; then conductor of the classical department of Antioch College, O., and at Eagleswood, N.J.; and is now Professor of Ancient Languages and History in Wisconsin University, Madison, Wis.

VI. **Ellis Allen** m., April 13, 1814, Lucy, daughter of Capt. Benjamin T. Lane, of Scituate. Their children were —

1. WILLIAM COWPER, b. Jan. 20, 1815.
2. GEORGE ELLIS, b. April 15, 1817.
3. JOSEPH ADDISON, b. April 25, 1819.
4. LUCY MARIA, b. Aug. 5, 1821.
5. NATHANIEL TOPLIFF, b. Sept. 29, 1823.
6. FANNY, b. Dec. 17, 1825; d. Oct. 17, 1831.
7. ABIGAIL ELLIS, b. May 17, 1828.
8. JAMES THEODORE, b. Aug. 29, 1831.

Grandchildren of ELLIS ALLEN, by his son WILLIAM COWPER: —

VII. **William Cowper** m. Harriet Coggin, of Mount Vernon, N.H., by whom he had ten children; viz.:

1. WILLIAM COGGIN, b. Oct. 23, 1844.
2. GEORGE ELLIS, b. April 3, 1846.
3. CHARLES THEODORE, b. Feb. 3, 1848.
4. HARRIET GRAZIELLA, b. Feb. 14, 1850.
5. NATHANIEL TOPLIFF, b. July 1, 1851.

6. ALPHONSO LAMARTINE, b. Feb. 19, 1854.
7. FRANK SHERWIN, b. Oct. 13, 1856.
8. JAMES FREDERIC, b. Feb. 28, 1858.
9. FANNY LOUISA, b. Jan. 29, 1860.
10. JOSEPH EDWARD, b. March 6, 1862.

William C. Allen, a machinist in Chicopee, now lives in Medfield. His wife, Harriet [Coggin], died suddenly, in Medfield, 1865.

VII. George Ellis m. Susan M. Treat, of Waltham; a teacher in West Newton and other places; now a teacher in the West Newton English and Classical School.

Their child, MINNIE TREAT ALLEN, was born March 27, 1860.

Grandchildren of ELLIS, by his son JOSEPH ADDISON:
VII. Joseph Addison m., Nov. 24, 1845, Lucy T., daughter of Aaron Burt, of Syracuse, N.Y., by whom he had three children: —

1. JOSEPH BURT, b. Jan. 2, 1852; d. Feb. 17, 1855.
2. ELLEN BURT, b. Dec. 19, 1855.
3. ROSA SMITH, b. Jan. 12, 1859.

Joseph Addison Allen, a teacher in Massachusetts, and in Syracuse, N.Y.; for about seven years, the Superintendent of the State Reform School in Westboro'; President of Normal and Training School, Fredonia, N.Y., from 1867 to 1869.

Grandchildren of ELLIS, by his daughter LUCY MARIA:
VII. Lucy Maria was a successful and favorite teacher in Northboro' and other towns; m., in 1842, James Davis, of Northboro'. Their children were —

1. JOSEPH ALLEN, b. Aug. 12, 1843. Killed in the battle of Chancellorsville, Va., 1863.
2. JAMES THROCKMORTON, b. Nov. 3, 1845; d. Aug. 5, 1847.

3. GEORGE DOLOR, b. Nov. 6, 1847.
4. FANNY EVA, b. Oct. 21, 1849.
5. ABBY ANNA, b. June 25, 1851.
6. CHARLES SEDGWICK, b. June 12, 1853.
7. LUCY ELLEN, b. March 22, 1855.
8. FREDERICK GALE, b. Aug. 13, 1862.

James Davis, with his wife Lucy Maria, lived first in Northboro'; afterwards, in Syracuse, N.Y.; afterwards, in Northboro', Medfield, and Fairhaven. He served in the Eleventh Massachusetts Battery in the late war. The remains of their son Joseph A. Davis were brought from Chancellorsville, and interred in the cemetery at Northboro'.

Grandchildren of ELLIS, by his son NATHANIEL TOPLIFF :

VII. Nathaniel Topliff m. Caroline S., daughter of James N. Bassett, of Nantucket. Their children were :
1. FANNY BASSETT, b. Feb. 21, 1857.
2. SARAH CAROLINE, b. April 12, 1861 [Fort Sumter].
3. NATHANIEL TOPLIFF, b. Aug. 25. 1864 ; d. April 25, 1865.
4. LUCY ELLIS, b. May 3, 1867.

NOTE. — N. T. Allen was a student at the Rensselaer Institute, Troy, N.Y., and graduated at the State Normal School, Bridgewater; was for six years Principal of the Model Department of the State Normal School at West Newton, the first ever established in this country ; established, and has been for the last fifteen years, Principal of the English and Classical School in West Newton.

VII. Abigail Ellis, daughter of Ellis Allen, m. Charles Dana Davis, of Northboro'.
They live at present in Syracuse, N Y.

VII. James Theodore, youngest son of Ellis Allen, m., 1860, Caroline A., daughter of Dr. Edward A. Kittredge, of Lynn. Their children were —

1: EDWARD ELLIS, b. Aug. 1, 1861.
2. JAMES THEODORE, b. March 26, 1863 ; d. Jan. 27, 1864.
3. FREDERICK CUNNINGHAM, b. Feb. 8, 1865.
4. JENNIE CLARK, b. Sept. 13, 1867.

NOTE. — James T. Allen was a graduate of the Normal School, Bridgewater; graduate and professor of the Rensselaer Institute, Troy, N.Y.; travelled two years in Europe and the East; at present, Associate Principal in the English and Classical School in West Newton.

VI. **Silas,** third son of Phineas and Ruth Allen, took the name of **William Winthrop** Allen. Graduated at Harvard College, 1817. Studied for the ministry. He lives in Medfield.

VI. **Asa Smith,** fourth son of Phineas and Ruth Allen, m. Lydia Kingsbury, of Walpole. Their children were —

1. FRANCES ABIGAIL, b. Walpole, Oct. 9, 1820 ; d. in Schuyler, N.Y., on their journey to Western New York, May 29, 1823.
2. THOMAS SCOTT, b. July 26, 1825.
3. FRANCES ABIGAIL, b. May 8, 1827.
4. GEORGIANA ASPASIA, b. Dec. 26, 1829.
5. RUTH ANN, b. in Angelica, N.Y., July 3, 1832.
6. WILLIAM WIRT, b. Angelica, July 29, 1834.
7. HARRIET ELIZABETH ATWOOD, b. July 19, 1837.
8. ALMA ANNETTE, b. May 3, 1840.
9. MARY ADNA, b. Jan. 6, 1845.
10. HARRIET ATWOOD, b. Dec. 14, 1822 ; d. in Cuba, N.Y., July 18, 1837. His wife Lydia died Aug. 14, 1847, in Dodgeville, Wis.; and, Oct. 2, 1850, he married Martha Jane [Barney] Camp,

widow of Albert Camp, the mother of five daughters. By his second wife, he had —

11. ALBERT BARNES, b. Sept. 9, 1851.
12. CLARA AUGUSTA, b. May 29, 1853.
13. NETTIE ANNIS, b. June 15, 1855.

By her first husband, Albert Camp, she had —

1. HELEN M., b. Oct. 17, 1840, in Rutland, Vt.
2. MARIETTA S., b. Jan. 10, 1842; m. George Wárner.
3. FLAVIA A., b. Jan. 28, 1844.
4. SARAH JANE, b. Oct. 16, 1845.
5. DELIA ANN, b. Nov. 27, 1847.

NOTE. — Asa S. Allen, at the age of twenty-two, was deacon of the Congregational Church, Walpole; removed, in 1823, to the new township of Andover, Alleghany County, New York; thence to Angelica, where he studied for the ministry, and, in 1836, was ordained over the church in Cuba, in the same county; removed, in 1846, to Dodgeville, Wis., and thence to Black Earth, in both which places he was pastor of a Congregational Church. He has since removed to Clear Lake, Io.

Of the children of Rev. ASA SMITH ALLEN, —

VII. **Thomas Scott** m., 1851, Sally Bracken, daughter óf General Bracken, by whom he had two children : one of whom died in infancy ; the other, Ellen Frances, b. Oct. 18, 1852. His wife died in 1854; m. again Miss Natalie, of Mineral Point.

NOTE. — Thomas Scott Allen studied at Oberlin College, Ohio; served, as an officer, in the Union army through the whole period of the Rebellion, rising from the rank of Captain to that of Brigadier-General; received several severe wounds; returned to his home in Wisconsin at the close of the war, and was elected Secretary of the State in 1865, which office he still retains. He now lives in Madison, Wis.

VII. **Frances Abigail** m. Samuel Grove, of Stockton, Cal., April 12, 1854. Her husband died in

1856. She went to California as a teacher, by
the Isthmus.

VII. **Georgiana Aspasia** went to California, by the over-
land route, in the same year and in the same
capacity; m., Nov. 16, 1854, William H. Lyons,
Esq., attorney-at-law in Stockton. Their children were —

1. FRANCES ALLEN, b. November, 1855.
2. WILLIAM HENRY, b. Dec. 30, 1857; d. 1858.
3. VIRGINIA, b. Aug. 14, 1859.
4. GEORGIA WASHINGTON, b. Feb. 22, 1862.

VII. **Ruth Ann,** teacher of Freedmen in Mobile, Ala.

VII. **William Wirt** m., in 1858, Selah Dennison, of Eau
Claire, Wis. They have two sons.

NOTE. — William Wirt was Hospital Steward in the Second Wisconsin Regiment, in which capacity, and as Assistant Surgeon, he
served his country through the war. He was taken prisoner in the
battle of Gainsville, Va. He is now a physician in Iowa.

VII. **Harriet Elizabeth Atwood** m. John Reid, of Stock-
ton, Cal., Aug. 21, 1862.
VII. **Alma Annette** m. Jan. 1, 1863, Elbert Smith, of
Stockton, Cal.

Harriet and Alma went to California as teachers.

VII. **Mary Adna** lives with her father in Iowa; as do
the three youngest children, — Albert Barnes,
Clara Augusta, and Nettie Annis.

VI. **Abigail,** daughter of Phineas and Ruth Allen, m.,
Nov. 11, 1818, Gershom Adams, of Medfield.
Their children were —

VII. **George Frederic,** b. July 27, 1820 ; m., April 29, 1841, Martha A. Barker.

NOTE. — George Frederic studied medicine ; served, as Surgeon in the First Brooklyn Regiment, through the war.

Their children were —

1. JAMES ROBERT, b. Oct. 10, 1846.
2. GEORGE FREDERIC, b. Jan. 29, 1849 ; d. Dec. 6, 1868.
3. CHARLES FREMONT, b. February, 1856.

VII. **Charles Edward,** b. Jan. 15, 1822, m. Jane Furman, of Syracuse, N.Y., April 4, 1848. Their children were —

1. ROBERT FURMAN, b. Dec. 23, 1848.
2. CHARLES STANLEY, b. July 23, 1853 ; d. March 4, 1855.
3. ANNABEL, b. April 13, 1862.
4. PRESTON MANN, b. April 28, 1868 ; d. Aug. 26, 1868.

NOTE. — Charles E. was first a teacher, afterwards a merchant, in New York.

VII. **John Quincy** b. July 7, 1824.

Lives in California.

VII. **James,** b. June 6, 1827; d. Jan. 2, 1846.
VII. **Robert Bruce,** b. Jan. 2, 1834 ; d. July 2, 1842.

VI. **Phineas Allen** graduated at Harvard College 1825; m., 1828, Clarissa Fiske, of Medfield. Their children were —

1. FRANCIS EUGENE, b. Feb. 27, 1830 ; d. May 2, 1830.
2. HORATIO FISKE, b. Aug. 4, 1831.
3. ROBERT ALFRED, b. July 29, 1833.

4. GEORGE EDGAR, b. March 2, 1838.
5. CHARLES EUGENE, b. July 20, 1841; d. Feb. 11, 1864.
6. CLARA EVERETT, b. Aug. 25, 1846.

Of these children of PHINEAS ALLEN, —

  Horatio F. m. Catherine Butterfield, of Tyngsborough, by whom he had —

1. MORTIMER BUTTERFIELD, b. Aug. 3, 1857.
2. ELIZABETH WHITTLE, b. Feb. 3, 1861.
3. EDGAR FISKE, b. May 8, 1862.

Horatio graduated at the Normal School, Bridgewater; teacher in Newtonville and other places. He now lives in Newtonville.

VII. Robert Alfred, son of Phineas Allen, m. Martha Turney, of Perry, Wyoming County, N.Y. He is at present an apothecary in Cleveland, O. Their children were —

1. MABEL, b. Jan. 15, 1860, at Syracuse, N.Y.
2. CHARLES FISKE.
3. ALFRED EUGENE, b. July 8, 1866, at Cleveland, O.

VII. George Edgar, son of Phineas Allen, m. Fanny Phillips. Their child, Frank Farnum, b. June 9, 1868, at Boston.

  Served in the navy through the war, as the second engineer of the " Underwriter."

VII. Charles Eugene, son of Phineas Allen. Returned, from a sea-voyage, to West Newton, in the winter of 1864, where he died Feb. 11 of that year.

VII. **Clara Everett,** only daughter of Phineas Allen, m. Charles Channcy Chamberlain. Has one child, Clara Elizabeth, b. April 4, 1868.

NOTE. — Phineas Allen, Jr., was for many years Principal of the Academy in Concord; afterwards, of the Academy in Northfield. At present, an assistant teacher in the English and Classical School in West Newton.

VI. **Noah Allen,** youngest son of Phineas and Ruth Allen, m. Paulina Sarah, daughter of Ruggles Whiting, Esq., of Dover, by whom he had three children : —

1. LUCIUS WHITING, b. Aug. 5, 1835.
2. HELEN ZENOBIA, b. March 22, 1838.
3. SARAH PAULINA, b. Aug. 2, 1842.

Of these children of NOAH, —

VII. **Lucius W.** m., Oct. 4, 1864, Almira F. Leeds, of Dorchester. He was one of the earliest voluu-teers in the late war ; and is now a clerk in the Post-offiee, Boston.

VII. **Helen Zoe,** a teacher in Medfield and Dover.

VII. **Sarah P.** m., Oct. 26, 1865, Jerome S. Daniels, of Franklin.

Lucius W. has one child, Paulina Florence, b. Dec. 6, 1866.

GENEALOGY OF ELEAZER, SON OF JOSEPH ALLEN.

It appears, from papers in my possession, that JOSEPH ALLEN, son of James, purchased a tract of land in the southerly part of Dover, for his oldest son, JOSEPH, but which came into the possession of ELEAZER, born in 1688. Eleazer m., July 9, 1712, Mary Battelle.

Their children were —

1. ELEAZER, Jr., 2. OBEDIAH, 3. SAMUEL, and 4.
MARY, baptized April 24, 1726; 5. ESTHER,
baptized May 30, 1731. — Church records of
Rev. Mr. Baxter.

IV. ELEAZER, Jr., by his wife Sibil, had one son and
three daughters : —

1. ELEAZER, 3d, m. Rebecca Mason.
2. AMY, unmarried; lived in Medfield.
3. PHEBE, m. Joseph Johnson.
4. SIBIL, m. Ephraim Wilson.

Of these children of ELEAZER, Jr., —

V. ELEAZER, by his wife Rebecca [Mason], had three
children : —

1. HITTY, m. Jesse Newell; lived in Dover.
2. JOHN, m. a daughter of Joseph Cheney, of Dover.
3. REBECCA.

VI. HITTY was the mother of nine children; viz. : —

1. REBECCA, died in her youth.
2. CHARLES, m. Mary Ann Partridge, of Medway.
3. JOHN A., m. Caroline, daughter of Colonel Obed
Allen.
4. AMY,   ⎫ died in their youth.
5. DOLLY,   ⎭
6. BETSEY, m. Obed Allen, Jr.
7. SARAH, m. Mason Brown.   Mother and child died.
8. HITTY, m. Sherman Battelle, Esq., of Dover.
9. JESSE, m. Pamela Cleaveland, who died in 1841;
m., about 1843, Lydia, widow of James Prince,
of Salem.

Of the children of JESSE and HITTY [ALLEN]
NEWELL, —

VII. Charles, by his wife Mary Ann, had two daughters,
ABIGAIL and MARTHA, and one son died in
infancy.

VII. John A., by his wife Caroline, had five children ; viz. : —

JOHN A., Jr., HARRIET, SARAH, WILLIAM, and CAROLINE.

Sarah died, with her first child.

VII. Hitty, by her husband, S. Battelle, Esq., had four children : —

1. ALLEN E., m. Marcia Bacon ; a Baptist minister.
2. MONROE, lives in the city of New York.
3. ANN JEANETTE, m. Rev. Timothy Bailey.
4. CATHERINE, m. Lawrence A. Derby, merchant in Elmira, N.Y.

VII. Jesse Newell, Jr., by his wife Pamela, had five children : —

1. LUCY MARIA, b. 1826, m. James H. Prince, engineer on Boston and Providence Railroad.
2. ELEAZER A., b. 1827, m. Elizabeth Thayer, Elmira, N.Y.
3. JESSE EMORY, b. 1830, engineer on a railroad in New York.
4. ANN, b. 1833, m. Hosea Towne, of Newton.
5. FRANCIS E., b. 1836, m. Sophia Hall, of Roxbury.

His wife Pamela died in 1842, and in 1843 he married Lydia N. Prince, of Medfield, by whom he had three children : —

6. DENZIL M., b. 1843.
7. EMMA P., b. 1845.
8. BETTY E., b. 1848.

NOTE. — Jesse Newell, Jr., lives on the old homestead in Dover.

GENEALOGY OF HEZEKIAH, SON OF JOSEPH AND HANNAH [SABINE] ALLEN, b. 1692.

III. **Hezekiah** was by trade a carpenter; lived first in Weston, afterwards in Dover, to which place he removed about 1715, and where he became the owner of a large tract of land extending from Natick to Medfield. By an instrument found among the papers belonging to the family, it appears that, in May, 1725, Hannah, widow of Joseph Allen, leased to her son Hezekiah twenty-five acres of land (part of her thirds) during her life, said land "lying in Dedham wood lot, called the Old Field, bounded north by land of said Hezekiah, and south by land of Eleazer Allen." The instrument contains the autographs of Hannah, Hezekiah, and Mary [probably the wife of Hezekiah].

A part of this large tract of land is still in the possession of descendants of the two brothers.

III. **Hezekiah,** by his wife [Mary?] had two children:
    1. HEZEKIAH, Jr., baptized by Rev. Joseph Baxter, Sept. 27, 1724.
    2. MARY, bap. Oct. 1, 1727.

IV. **Hezekiah, Jr.,** married, in 1743, a Miss Kingsbury, of Needham, by whom he had five children, two of whom died in infancy. Three had families, and lived to old age; viz.: —
    1. TIMOTHY.
    2. RACHEL. } Of these two daughters, I have no ac-
    3. JEMIMA. } count.

V. **Timothy,** son of Hezekiah, Jr., m. Rebecca Eames, by whom he had four sons and two daughters; viz.: —

1. HEZEKIAH, b. Dec. 12, 1775; d. Nov. 18, 1858, in Orange, N.J.
2. POLLY, b. Dec. 31, 1778; m. John N. Sumner, Ashford, Conn.
3. THADDEUS, b. May 14, 1780; m. Clarissa Bullard.
4. TIMOTHY, Jr., b. May 19, 1782; m. Abigail Fisher, of Dover.
5. REBECCA, b. May 20, 1784; m. Ebenezer Smith, Dover.
6. JARED, b. April 11, 1789; m. Hannah Richards.

Of these children of TIMOTHY, the eldest,

VI. 𝕳𝖊𝖟𝖊𝖐𝖎𝖆𝖍, m., in 1802, Julia Whiting, by whom he had —

1. ALMIRA, m. Leonard Perry, a merchant in Baltimore.
2. JULIA, m. Rev. P. R. Minard, St. Louis.
3. CATHERINE, d. in Dover, Oct. 8, 1829.
4. HARRIET, d. in St. Louis, Sept. 26, 1838.
5. ALLSTON, m., June 5, 1833, Eliza R. Ordway, merchant, Orange, N.J.
6. HANNAH ELLIS, m. Luther W. Mason, professor of music in Cincinnati, Ohio.

The children of Almira are Mary Jones, Allston Allen, and George Leonard. Allston Allen Perry is a merchant in South Natick; a daughter of Julia, Catherine E., lives in Baltimore.

1208977

VII. Allston, the fifth child and only son of Hezekiah, by his wife Eliza Richards Allen, had six children; viz.: —

1. JULIA MINARD, b. Feb. 6, 1836; m. Charles C. Hutchinson.
2. HARRIET, b. Aug. 18, 1838.
3. MARY ORDWAY, b. Oct. 24, 1840.

4. FRANK ALLSTON, b. Dec. 2, 1843.
5. CATHERINE TRACEY, b. July 8, 1847.
6. ELEANOR EUSTIS, b. Jan. 17, 1850.

Hannah E., the youngest child of Hezekiah, had four children, — Henry, Mary, Almira Virginia, and Catherine.

VI. **Timothy Allen, Jr.,** grandson of Hezekiah, Jr., by his wife Abigail, had four children; viz.:
1. LUCY FISHER, died in 1855.
2. FISHER AMES, married Mrs. Mary Cole; lives in Charlestown.
3. SAMUEL FISHER, m. Hannah Ellis, West Dedham.
4. TIMOTHY, m. Sarah Richardson, Dover.

VI. **Thaddeus Allen,** by his second wife, Ann Hunt [Ballard], had three sons and two daughters. Two are not living. The three living children are —
1. JOSEPH HUNT, b. Feb. 19, 1817; m. Matilda, C. Fearing. Lives in Boston; editor.
2. JAMES BALLARD, m. Ellen Simonds.
3. ELIZABETH C., lives in Boston.

Another daughter, Clarissa B., m. David Tyler, of Readville.

VII. **Joseph Hunt Allen** has one son and one daughter living: —
1. JOSEPH MARSHALL.
2. ANNIE MATILDA.

VI. **Jared Allen,** another son of Timothy, Jr., had a son and a daughter; viz.: —
1. JARED, Jr.
2. POLLY.

VII. **Jared Allen, Jr.,** besides a child who died in infancy, had also a son and a daughter; viz. : —

1. MARTHA BIRD, m. John P. Bachelder, of Dover.
2. SUMNER STANLEY, m. Eliza B. Gilman.

VI. **Polly,** daughter of Jared Allen, Sr., m. John N. Sumner; was the mother of five children; viz.:

1. BRIDGET P., died at Ashford, Conn.
2. MARY, m. Dr. Samuel Bowen, of Thomson, Conn.
3. JOHN NEWMAN, m. Deborah Fuller, of Montrose, Penn.
4. TIMOTHY ALLEN, m. Caroline Bates, of Boston.
5. BENJAMIN, m. Susan W. Lyon, of Woodstock, Conn.

VII. The daughters of **Mary** and Dr. Bowen are —

1. MARY HELEN, m. S. R. Harlow, of Kingston, N.J.
2. SARAH JANE, died at the age of 16.

VII. The children of **John Newman Sumner,** besides two daughters who died in infancy, are : —

1. JOHN.
2. ALFRED WRIGHT, lives at Seneca Falls, N.Y.

VII. **Timothy Allen Sumner,** by his wife Caroline, had one son : —

ALLEN MELANCTHON, b. Jan. 31, 1844.

VII. **Benjamin,** by his wife Susan W., has two children:

1. WILLIAM LYON. } They live in Woodstock,
2. GARDNER HIBBARD. } Conn.

VI. **Rebecca,** daughter of Timothy, by his first wife, Rebecca Eames, m. Ebenezer Smith, Jr., of Dover [b. Feb. 27, 1779; d. April 27, 1848].

Their children were eight, — six sons and two daughters ; viz. : —

1. MELANCTHON, a merchant, died in Jamaica Plain, July 10, 1861.
2. REBECCA EANES.
3. ORLANDO.
4. REUBEN, died in infancy.
5. LUCIUS, a farmer ; lives in Dover.
6. CLARA ALLEN, m. David Ellis Allen.
7. ABNER LEWIS.
8. WILLIAM FRANCIS, m. Caroline S. Cobb ; lives in Cleveland, O.

VII. Melancthon m. Lucy Ann Hunt, and is the father of —

1. EDWARD MELANCTHON, a broker in Jamaica Plain.
2. MARY ASHTON, m. Samuel T. Holmes.

IV. Hezekiah Allen, Jr., by his second wife, Mary [Peters], had ten children ; viz. : —

1. CALLA, b. Jan. 11, 1759 ; m. Isaiah Smith, of Medfield.
2. ZILLAH, b. Sept. 4, 1760 ; unmarried.
3. HEZEKIAH PETERS, b. May 3, 1762 ; m. Miss Thomas, of Maine.
4. PEREZ, b. Feb. 7, 1764 ; m. Hitta Richards.
5. WILLIAM PITT, b. Oct. 21, 1766 ; m. Keziah Mason, of Medfield.
6. HITTA, died in infancy.
7. CALVIN, b. March 1, 1770 ; m. Abigail Richards.
8 and 9. POLLY and PATTY, twins, b. March 11, 1763. Polly died young ; Patty m. Moses Fisher.
10. MORRILL ALLEN, b. April 3, 1776 ; m., May 14, 1801, Hannah Dean.

NOTE. — Rev. Morrill Allen graduated at Brown University, R.I., in 1798. He is still living in Pembroke, Mass., at the great age of 93. He preached a sermon on his 90th birthday.

V. **William P.**, by his wife Keziah [Mason], had seven children : —

1. REUBEN, b. Sept. 13, 1789 ; m. Mary B. Shedd.
2. WILLARD, d. in infancy.
3. WILLARD, b. Aug. 5, 1793 ; lived in Deerfield, Mass.
4. MARTHA, b. Jan. 3, 1796 ; m. Ralph Battelle.
5. IRA, b. July 11, 1797 : m., first, Pamela Whitney ; second, Esther Townsend.
6. AMOS, b. Oct. 18, 1799 ; m. Adaline Goodenough, of Natick.
7. MARY, b. March 14, 1802 : m., first, Capt. Brett ; second, Deacon Capen, of Canton.

Reuben had one child, Mary Ann.

VII. **Mary Ann,** b. April 10, 1812 ; m. Elias Haskett Derby, whose children were —

1. SARAH ELLEN ; m. William Rogers.
2. RICHARD, b. Oct. 3, 1834.
3. PICKMAN, died at the age of six years.

NOTE. — Richard Derby was a captain in the Fifteenth Regiment of Massachusetts Volunteers, and was instantaneously killed, while leading on his men, at the battle of Antietam.

VI. **Willard,** son of William Pitt Allen, lived in Deerfield, Mass. His children were —

1. WILLARD MASON, b. April 2, 1819.
2. MARTHA M., b. Feb. 23, 1821.
3. AMOS MORRILL, b. March 31, 1823.
4. GEORGE NETTLETON, b. July 7, 1825.
5. ELIJAH CRANE, b. Sept. 20, 1827.
6. ELIZABETH, b. Aug. 7, 1831.
7. WILLIAM PITT, b. March 10, 1835.

GENEALOGY OF REV. MORRILL ALLEN.

V. **Morrill Allen,** by his wife Hannah [Dean],
had ten children ; viz. : —

1. George Minot, b. Feb. 19, 1802 ; m. Hannah E.
   Otis.
2. Hannah C. D., b. Oct. 25, 1810 ; m. Dauphin
   King.
3. William Paley, b. Sept. 27, 1815 ; m. Abigail
   E. Otis.
4. Henry Ware, b. April 6, 1822 ; m. Amelia Colman.
5. Martha Jane, b. Aug. 10, 1826 ; m. William F.
   Wheeler, of Lincoln.

Of the other five children of Rev. M. Allen, I have
received no account. I suppose that they died in infancy.

VI. **George Minot,** by his wife Hannah E. [Otis],
had —

1. Hannah Dean, b. February, 1829 ; m. Rev. Jen-
   nings M. Milton, of Troy, Ohio.
2. Cornelia Maria, b. July, 1830 ; ⎫ live with their
3. George Otis, b. May, 1833 ;   ⎬ parents in
   Pembroke.   ⎭

Hannah C. D. has one child : —

VII. **Allen King,** b. November, 1841 ; an instructor in
music.

VI. **William Paley,** by his wife Abigail E. [Otis],
had eight children : —

1. Sarah Byran, b. February, 1839 ; an operator
   in a telegraph offiee, Boston.

    2. MARY LOUISA died young.

    3. WILLIAM HENRY, b. August, 1843 ; in a telegraph office, New York.

    4. JAMES OTIS, b. April, 1846 ; a sailor.

    5. FLORA THOMAS, b. December, 1848 ; a teacher.

    6. AMY FRANCES, b. September, 1851.

    7. FRANK BLAKE, b. October, 1853.

    8. NELLIE WEST, b. September, 1856.

VI. **Henry Ware**, another son of Rev. Morrill Allen, had six children ; viz. : —

    1. MARY, died in infancy.

    2. HENRY MORRILL, b. September, 1856.

    3. CHARLES, b. December, 1858.

    4. HORACE COLMAN, b. September, 1860.

    5. FLORA PAMELA, b. October, 1862.

    6. EMMA, b. September, 1864.

DESCENDANTS OF NEHEMIAH, YOUNGEST SON OF JOSEPH, AND GRANDSON OF JAMES, ALLEN.

III. **Nehemiah** had eight sons and one daughter ; viz. : —

    1. ELIPHALET, b. about 1728.

    2. NEHEMIAH, b. about 1730 ; d. March 26, 1822, aged 92.

    3. JOHN, b. about 1732.

    4. JACOB, b. Feb. 24, 1734 ; removed to Whitehall, New York.

    5. ABEL, b. March 3, 1736 ; d. 1820, aged 84.

    6. DAVID.

    7. TIMOTHY, m. Hannah Moffit.

8. ABIGAIL, b. Dec. 23, 1741; m. Aaron, son of
Isaac Allen.

9. ABNER, b. about 1743.

IV. **Eliphalet,** son of Nehemiah, had three sons and
one daughter; viz.: —

1. ELIJAH, b. April 10, 1765; d. April 19, 1843,
aged 78.

2. WILLARD, b. Aug. 14, 1770.

3. EDMUND.

4. RHODA, m. Caleb, son of Isaac Allen.

V. **Elijah,** son of Eliphalet, by his wife Lettice Hitchcock, had —

1. HANNAH, b. July 25, 1794.

2 and 3. LEMUEL and SANDERS, twins, b. April 14,
1796.

4. HARRIET, b. Aug. 1, 1798.

5. ELIJAH, b. Jan. 9, 1800; d. June 25, 1813.

V. **Willard,** another son of Eliphalet, by his wife
Hepsibah, had six children; viz.: —

1. JONATHAN, b. June 13, 1789.

2. CALVIN, b. July 22, 1791.

3. FRANCIS D., b. March 13, 1796; m. Olive Kingsbury.

4. CANDACE, b. June 5, 1803.

5. BOSTWICK, b. Feb. 7, 1808·

6. NATHANIEL, b. Feb. 27, 1810.

Willard removed with all his family, except Francis D.,
to Remsen, N.Y., of whom we have no further account.

VI. **Francis D.,** son of Willard Allen, had five children; viz.: —

1. CLARINDA, b. April 14, 1824.

2. ALFRED W., b. Jan. 28, 1827 ; d. Feb. 15, 1858.
3. JAMES, b. Dec. 28, 1831 ; d. Oct. 21, 1847.
4. WILLIAM, b. Oct. 10, 1835 ; lives in Boston.
5. MARY, b. Dec. 15, 1838 ; m. Mr. Perry, of Sturbridge.

VI. **Sanders,** twin-son of Elijah, grandson of Eliphalet Allen, m. Judith Boyd, by whom he had four children ; viz. : —
1. EMILY, b. Jan. 25, 1820.
2. ELIJAH, b. Sept. 17, 1822 ; lives in Brimfield.
3. GEORGE S., b. Aug. 1, 1827.
4. HENRY A., b. Feb. 6, 1836.

VII. **Henry A.** m. Phebe E. Warner, and lives in Brimfield.

VI. **Lemuel,** twin-brother of Sanders, m. Elvira Baker. Their children are —
1. CAROLINE E., b. May 28, 1821.
2. OTIS N., b. Dec. 19, 1825 ; d. in 1855.
3. MASSENA B., b. Aug. 5, 1828.

Elvira, the mother of these children, d. Aug. 26, 1831 ; and their father m. Luthera W. Woods, by whom he had —
4. ELVIRA M., b. March 12, 1835.
5. MERRICK W., b. Feb. 27, 1837.

Massena B. m. Olive H. Henry, of Brimfield.

This completes the account of the descendants of Eliphalet, the eldest son of Nehemiah.

Nehemiah, the second son of Nehemiah, Sr., lived in Sturbridge, and died in 1822, aged 92.

𝕵𝖔𝖍𝖓, third son of Nehemiah, m. Elizabeth, daughter of Isaac Allen; had seven children, — ELIZABETH, MIRIAM, MOSES, JOHN, WATERS, MARY, and SIMEON.

Simeon, b. 1787, m. a Miss Boyd, and d. July 4, 1844.

V. 𝕸𝖔𝖘𝖊𝖘, oldest son of John, by his wife Olive, had two sons and three daughters. The sons were Lorenzo and Alvord, of whom we have no account.

V. 𝕮𝖆𝖕𝖙𝖆𝖎𝖓 𝕾𝖎𝖒𝖊𝖔𝖓 𝕬𝖑𝖑𝖊𝖓, another son of John, had five children : —

1. SOPHRONIA, b. Nov. 16, 1809 ; d. in 1844.
2. MARIEL, b. Oct. 23, 1811.
3. 𝕵𝖔𝖍𝖓 𝕭., b. Oct. 12, 1813 ; a clergyman in Brookline, Ohio.
4. CHARLES N., b. Sept. 4, 1815 ; m. Elizabeth Hooker.
5. GEORGE SUMNER, b. 1808 ; d. in 1812.

VI. 𝕮𝖍𝖆𝖗𝖑𝖊𝖘 𝕹., by his wife Elizabeth, had seven children : —

1. JANE E., b. Aug. 31, 1838 ; d. 1853.
2. JOHN B., b. June 27, 1841.
3. CHARLOTTE A., b. Sept. 3, 1843.
4. JOSIE M., b. May 5, 1846.
5. ABBY B., b. Sept. 13, 1849 ; not living.
6. LIZZIE J. ; died in infancy.
7. LIZZIE B., b. Feb. 11, 1857.

IV. 𝕵𝖆𝖈𝖔𝖇, fourth son of Nehemiah, had four children :

1. JACOB, m. Polly Corban in 1783.
2. ABRAHAM, b. December, 1764 ; m. Hannah Newell, daughter of General Timothy Newell ; d. April, 1845.
3. EPHRAIM, b. March 10, 1766 ; m. Miriam, daughter of General T. Newell.
4. SYBIL.

V. **Jacob Allen, Jr.**, had six children; viz.: —

1. AMASA, b. Feb. 7, 1784.

NOTE. — Amasa was a physician in Whitehall, N.Y.; studied medicine with his uncle, Dr. Abram Allen, of Salem, N.Y.; graduated at the Medical College, Castleton, Vt.; d. Nov. 5, 1830.

2. LUCY, b. Jan. 23, 1786; m. Phineas Walker, of Woodstock, Conn.
3. ELECTA, b. Jan. 1, 1789; m. Charles Hobbs, of Sturbridge.
4. MARIA, b. Feb. 15, 1796; m. S. D. Phelps, of Fitchburg.
5. ELVIRA, b. March 17, 1798; m. Samuel Standish, of North Granville, N.Y.
6. MARY, b. Jan. 24, 1800; m. Dr. Benjamin D. Utter, of Whitehall. They now live in Amsterdam, N.Y.

VI. **Dr. Amasa Allen,** by his wife Fanny Steel, had three children: —

1. RICHARD S., b. Nov. 9, 1814; m. Ann Eliza Dupuy, of Elkton, Ala.
They have six children, who live in Vaiden, Carrol Co., Miss.
2. HORACE S., b. Aug. 14, 1818; m. Mary A. Lightbody, and lives in Jersey City, doing business in New York.
3. MARY, b. May 16, 1823; m. Michael J. Myers, of Whitehall, N.Y. They now live in Poughkeepsie, N.Y.

VI. **Lucy,** daughter of Jacob Allen, Jr., had thirteen children, — six sons and seven daughters, — nine of whom are supposed to be still living, some in Illinois and others in Massachusetts.

VI. **Electa** had two daughters, who married, the one
R. N. Mason, the other Ezra Dean, of Woodstock, Conn.   Electa is still living.

VI. **Maria** had one daughter, now Mrs. Bronson.

VI. **Elvira** has no children.

VI. **Mary** has one son and one daughter.

V. **Abraham,** son of Jacob Allen, Sr., had two sons,
who died young.

NOTE.—Abraham was eminent in his profession, especially as a
surgeon.

V. His brother **Ephraim** had six sons and one daughter : —

1. **Timothy Newell,** b. in Monson, March 31, 1794 ;
m. Catherine Finn, of Fort Edward, N.Y.; d.
1826, in the first year of his law-practice.

2. **Henry,** b. in Monson, Nov. 29, 1795 ; m. Chris-
tiana Robinson, at Fort Miller, N.Y.; d. at
Whitehall, 1849, leaving his widow and two
sons, Henry and Charles.

3. **Charles,** b. at Salem, N.Y., Sept. 27, 1797 ; d.
at Whitehall, March, 1852, leaving a daughter,
since deceased.

4. **Jacob,** b. Oct. 3, 1802 ; lives in Buffalo, and has
two daughters.

5. **George,** a physician, b. Jan. 12, 1806 ; m. Caroline Harvey; d. 1865, leaving three sons and
one daughter, — viz., Charles H. [a physician],
George, James H., and Caroline.

6. **William Pitt,** b. Feb. 14, 1808 ; m. Harmion
Smith, at Hartford, N.Y.; d. at Whitehall,
N.Y., 1854, leaving his widow, and a son and
a daughter, William Pitt and Caroline.

7. **Caroline,** b. March 11, 1799 ; m. Dr. Archibald
McAllister ; had seven children, of whom Miriam and Sarah only are living. Their residence
is in Salem, N.Y.

VI. **Abel,** fifth son of Nehemiah, had five children ; viz. :

1. ABEL, b. March 30, 1767 ; m. Experience Parker,
in 1792.
2. ALFRED, b. April 24, 1768 ; m. Lucebia Ballard,
in 1791.
3. EZRA, b. Sept. 6, 1773 ; m. Mary M. Needham,
in 1802.
4. JERUSHA, b. Sept. 12, 1775 ; m. James Lynn, d.
1865.
5. ESTHER, b. Oct. 2, 1784 ; m. Captain Freeland
Wallis.

V. **Abel Allen, Jr.,** had six children ; viz. : —

1. HARMONIA, b. Dec. 26, 1793 ; d. in 1844.
2. HORACE, b. May 2, 1796 ; m. Maria Upham, d. in
1852.
3. ADALINE A., b. June 20, 1801.
4. BETSEY, b. June 9, 1805.
5. HARRIET, b. Oct. 8, 1807 ; m. Jesse B. Adams,
Grass Lake, Mich.
6. CHARLES G., b. March 5, 1809 ; m. Mary Dunton.

VI. **Charles G. Allen,** son of Abel Allen, Jr., had
three children ; viz. : —

1. CHARLES H., b. Sept. 21, 1837.
2. JULIA D., b. Dec. 7, 1840.
3. MARY A., b. Nov. 26, 1846.
The family live in Sturbridge.

V. **Alfred,** second son of Abel Allen, Sr., had seven
children ; viz. : —

1. AUGUSTA, b. Feb. 24, 1793; m. N. C. Martin, of
   Milton.
2. ORESTES, b. Nov. 27, 1795; m. Lavinia Lilley, of
   Homer, N.Y.
3. PLINY, b. Feb. 18, 1799; m. Elvira Norcross,
   merchant in Monson.
4. PARSONS, b. Feb. 16, 1802; m. Lucy Brown;
   lives in Brimfield.
5. CHENEY BULLARD, b. September, 1805; m. A. A.
   Winship, merchant in Boston.
6. ESTHER LUCEBIA, b. Sept. 9, 1810; m. J. P. Cur-
   tis, who died in Louisville, Ky.   His widow
   now lives in Westboro'.
7. NORMAN W., b. Oct. 9, 1812; d. 1816.

VI. **Parsons,** fourth child of Alfred, had three sons;
   viz. : —

1. EDWIN B., b. June 29, 1831; m. Sabina Fuller;
   d. 1859.
2. DWIGHT P., b. April 22, 1832; m. Josephine
   Shaw.
3. GEORGE G., b. Jan. 18, 1840; merchant in Chi-
   cago.

VII. **Edwin B.** has one son, Harlem P., b. Nov. 11, 1856.

VII. **Dwight P.** has one son, Waldo B.; lives in Brimfield.

V. **Col. Ezra Allen,** third son of Abel Allen, Sr.,
   had four children : —

1. MARY C., b. Nov. 12, 1804; m. Trueman Charles.
2. ROXANA, b. Aug. 24, 1809; m. Joseph Stone, d.
   Feb. 12, 1868.
3. HARRISON, b. April 18, 1814; m. Harriet A. Partridge.
4. JOSEPH L., b. Sept. 24, 1815; m. Phebe S. Partridge.

Of these children of Colonel Ezra, the youngest,

VI. **Joseph Lathrop** had five children, two dying
in infancy.

1. CYNTHIA P., b. June, 1840 ; m. George Homer, of
Boston.
2. LIZZIE M., b. Jan. 1845.
3. MARY C., b. April, 1848.

Colonel Ezra lived in Holland, Mass., where he died
Oct. 30, 1866, aged 93. He told me, in 1865, that he dis-
tinctly remembered his grandfather, Nehemiah, who came
from Medfield.

Of **David,** sixth son of Nehemiah, we have no record.

IV. **Timothy,** seventh son of Nehemiah Allen, had six
children ; viz. : —

1. SABINE, b. July 6, 1769 ; m. Anne Corbin.
2. PARKER, d., in Sturbridge, about 1836 ; unmarried.
. MATILDA, m. Simeon Rice, of Brookfield.
3. HANNAH, m. Dwight Johnson.
5. HEZEKIAH, b. Feb. 15, 1781 ; m. Lucinda Walker ;
d. 1863.
6. TIMOTHY, b. June, 1788 ; m. Clarissa Marsh.

V. **Sabine,** son of Timothy, had five children, viz. :

1. CHLOE, b. April 7, 1793 ; m. Benjamin Burnham.
Their children were Austin Allen, Louisa, Benjamin, and Betsey.
2. NEHEMIAH, b. Sept. 17, 1795 ; m. Hannah Dun-
ham. Their children were Alson, Hezekiah,
Lucinda, James, John M., and Warren.
Warren lives in Danville, Dodge Co., Miss.
3. NANCY, b. May 14, 1799 ; m. Salmon P. Abell.
Their children were Corbin Allen, Volney V.,

Rodney C., and Caroline.   Corbin A. d. 1850.
Volney V. d. 1864.   The other two are living.

4. CORBIN, b. May 24, 1803; m. Elvira Beebee.   His
children were James Sabine, who died, on his
way to California, in 1850, and Corbin, supposed to be living in Kansas.

5. LOUISA, b. Nov. 22, 1806; m. John D. Nelson, of
West Haven, Vt.

Sabine, the father of these five children, lived in White-
hall, N.Y.   Removed to Dresden, N.Y., where he died
Sept. 11, 1824.   Of the other children of Timothy Allen,
Sr., except Timothy, we have no record.

V. **Col. Timothy Allen,** youngest son of Timothy, had five children : —

1. MATILDA, b. May, 1813; lives in Brookfield, N.Y.
2. CAROLINE, b. July, 1817.
3. WINTHROP M., b. 1819; lives in Brookfield, N.Y.
4. GEORGE, b. February, 1821; lives in Wisconsin.
5. CLEMENTINE, b. September, 1823; lives in Wisconsin.

Col. Timothy Allen removed from Sturbridge first to
Brookfield, N.Y.; thence to Green Bay, Wis., where he
died in 1857.

IV. **Abner,** youngest son of Nehemiah, had six children : —

1. PENUEL, b. Oct. 17, 1772.
2. JEMIMA, b. Sept. 3, 1774.
3. HENRY, b. Nov. 2, 1776; m. Mary Smith in 1801.
4. STEPHEN, b. May 9, 1781.
5. ABNER, b. Oct. 31, 1782.
6. THENA, b. Oct. 15, 1787; m. Salem Charles, of
Sturbridge.

Abner, the father of these six children, d. March 7, 1830,
aged 87.   Deborah, his wife, d. May 13, 1821.

V. **Henry,** the third child of Abner, had five children :

1. Mercy, b. Jan. 13, 1802.
2. Laurinda, b. July 6, 1804 ; m. Merrick Cheney, of Union, Conn.
3. Augusta, b. July 22, 1806 ; m. Joseph Gifford, of East Hartford, Conn.
4. Liberty, b. Sept. 11, 1809 ; m. Elizabeth Aldrich, in 1833.
5. Pamela, b. June 11, 1812 ; m. Levi Reed, of Union, Conn.

VI. **Liberty,** the only son of Henry, had eight children ; viz. : —

1. Laurinda E., b. June 30, 1837.
2. William L., b. Dec. 17, 1838.
3. Joel H., b. March 24, 1840 ; died young.
4. Mary L., b. April 25, 1843.
5. Giles Waldo, b. Dec. 1, 1844.
6. Julia E., b. June 17, 1846.
7. Adelaide M., b. July 9, 1851.
8. Caroline A., b. Feb. 11, 1854.

Giles Waldo enlisted in the war of the Rebellion, was taken prisoner, confined in Salisbury Prison, and died soon after his return home, March, 1865, from the effects of ill-treatment and starvation.

Liberty Allen lives on the old homestead in Sturbridge, where had lived his father Henry and his grandfather Abner.

IV. **Abigail,** only daughter of Nehemiah, who was married to Aaron, son of Isaac Allen, had eleven children : —

1. Reuben, b. 1764; d., in Sturbridge, in 1818.
2. Amy, b. 1766 ; died young.
3. Sibbil, b. 1768.
4. Lois, b. 1770.

5. KIAS, b. 1772; m. Polly Bracket.   He died in
    1851; she, in 1849.
6. BETSEY, b. 1774.
7. ETHAN, b. 1776; d. 1811.
8. MARY, b. 1778.
9. AARON, b. 1781; d. 1818.
10. NABBY, b. 1783; d. 1787.
11. AMY, b. 1787.

Of these eleven children of Abigail, the eldest,

V. **Reuben** had six children; viz. : —

1. PERLEY, b. June 1, 1792; d. Oct. 22, 1865; dea-
    con of the Congregational Church in Sturbridge.
2. ABIGAIL, b. 1794; m. Silas Marsh.
3. REUBEN, b. 1798; d. 1803.
4. MELVIN, b. 1800; m. Sally Upham.
5. LUTHER, b. 1802; d. 1863.
6. ELVIRA, b. 1805.

V. **Kias,** another son of Abigail and Aaron Allen, had
    five children : —

1. ARVINA, b. 1807.
2. REUBEN, b. 1809; m. Harriet J. Moore.
3. ETHAN, b. 1813; m. Mary E. Kimball.
4. ORRIN, b. 1816; died in infancy.
5. AARON, b. 1820.

I give below another account of the descendants of Abigail and Aaron Allen, furnished me by Benjamin D. Allen,
of Worcester, one of their lineal descendants.

IV. **Abigail,** by her husband Isaac Allen, had eight
    children : —

1. AARON, whose children were Reuben, Ethan,
    Aaron, Betsey, Lois, and Amy.

2. SIMEON, m. Sarah Puffer, whose daughter Desire m. William Lombard.

3. ITHAMAR, had four children, — Nathan, Richard, Amy, and Dolly.

4. CALEB, m. Rhoda Allen. Their children were five, — Delight, Arba, Albon, Adassa, and Pallace.

5. ELISHA.

6. ELIZABETH, m. John Allen.

7. PRUDENCE, m. Mark Stacey.

8. THANKFUL.

Of these eight children, the fifth,

V. **Elisha** had eight children; viz.: —

1. OREN, b. April 10, 1786; d. Jan. 31, 1814; a physician in Warren.

2. WALTER, b. March 22, 1788; m. Harriet Holbrook, d. May 11, 1833.

3. THANKFUL, b. July 22, 1790; lives in Worcester.

4. CYLENDA, b. April 6, 1792; d. Oct. 5, 1826.

5. CALISTA, b. Nov. 10, 1795; m. Pardon Thompson, of Manlius, N.Y. Calista died July 7, 1831.

6. ALVAN, b. Nov. 13, 1798; m. Lucy Salisbury. Lived in Worcester; where' he died Nov. 29, 1859.

7. MARTHA B., b. Dec. 20, 1800; m. Alfred Hitchcock, of Brimfield.

8. ELISHA DWIGHT, b. March 27, 1804; m. Orril Merrick.

Of these eight, Dr. Oren Allen was never married. Walter had two sons, Dwight and George, the former of whom had eight children, — Caroline, Mary, Frederic, Francis, Alfred, Martha, Charles, and Mary: the latter, George, had six; viz., Mary, Dwight, Charles, George, Julia, and John.

VI. **Alvan,** the sixth child of Elisha, had two sons; viz.: —

1. ALBERT S., m. Eliza A. Cole, whose children are two, — Charles Albert and Mary Salisbury.
2. BENJAMIN D. ALLEN, m. Eliza F. White. Their children are Mabel, James White, Eliza Salisbury, and Charlotte Joy.

VI. **Martha B.** has two children, George M. and Laura A.

VI. **Elisha D.,** youngest son of Elisha Allen, had five children, — Alfred [in the U.S.N.], Charles D., Caroline M., Mary E. T., and Martha L.; m. Edward Fay, of Cambridgeport.

GOLDEN WEDDING OF ELLIS AND LUCY ALLEN.

Yours truly
Ellis Allen

ACCOUNT

OF THE

CELEBRATION OF THE GOLDEN WEDDING OF ELLIS AND LUCY ALLEN.

IT had long been the intention of the children of ELLIS and LUCY ALLEN to celebrate, in an appropriate manner, the Golden Wedding of their parents. Accordingly, an invitation was extended to numerous members of the family to repair to the old homestead, which has been in the uninterrupted possession of the Allens through seven generations, and assist in the ceremonies.

As it was found impossible to include all the relatives on both sides of the house, the invitation was limited to the immediate descendants, and to the brothers and sisters of the Bride and Bridegroom, with their families. Among these, some were in California, some on the Mississippi, and some serving their country in the army and navy. Altogether, the number of invitations given was over four hundred.

A heavy snow-storm set in, the day before the wedding; and its severity was such, that many friends were prevented from being present, while some drove

as much as twenty-five miles in an open sleigh. The
unpromising weather, however, was not allowed to in-
terrupt the preparations for the ceremonies; and the
daughters of the house were busy, for several days,
decking its antique rooms in robes of velvet moss and
trailing evergreen. One particular apartment, divested
of its modern furnishings, was made the receptacle of
sundry heirlooms. The black-visaged stove gave place
to the cheerful light of a blazing fire of wood, piled upon
brass-knobbed andirons; and the blackened crane,
with its pot-hooks of varying lengths, and singing tea-
kettle, recalled the scenes of bygone days. Tallow
candles, in shining candlesticks, with their accompany-
ing snuffers, adorned the shelf; while over the mantel
was hung a musket bearing date 1770, and, though
years of rust had dimmed its early lustre, it was all
aglow with memories of Bunker Hill and Lexington.
An ancient tea-sett, dating back four generations, was
displayed upon the wooden shelves; and ranged beside
it were the pewter plates, whose brightness was the
pride of the ancient housekeeper. The spinning-wheel
and its accompaniments graced the room, as of old;
and rich ears of corn, with braided husks, hung on the
walls. Straight-backed chairs — and one particular
rocker, which had lulled to infant slumber not a few of
the Allens — helped to complete the furnishing of this
really ancient room.

At ten o'clock of the eventful day, the guests began
to assemble, and were cordially received by William C.,
the oldest son of the house. An hour was spent in
social interchange, and the presentations of many beautiful and useful gifts, which quite overloaded the old-

fashioned table, itself a part of the simple outfit of the
bride of fifty years ago.

At half-past eleven, the meeting was called to order
by George E., the second son, who acted as master of
ceremonies, and who welcomed the friends in the following address : —

"MY FRIENDS, — We have assembled beneath the
hospitable roof of this old family mansion, this 'Home'
of the Allens, to celebrate the 'Golden Wedding' of
our honored parents ; and I desire for myself, but more
especially for them, to bid you a cordial, hearty welcome.

"We trust you have brought to-day joyous and gladsome spirits, for we desire to make the occasion one of
rejoicing ; and, though sad reminiscences may unbidden
well up from hearts overflowing with gratitude, let
them serve only as the shading of the picture, to
heighten and render more apparent its beauties. The
Bride and Groom of April 11, 1814, are of the sixth
generation of Allens who have owned and occupied this
ancestral estate, and they greet to-day, under its ample
roof, almost an unbroken family of children, — no absent one save a loved daughter, who died in youth ;
and who can say but her sweet spirit, so early transplanted, hovers around us at this moment, bringing
down the benediction of heaven, to hallow and purify
our joy ! Five brothers and one sister of the family of
the Groom, the youngest of whom bears upon his head
the frosts of more than threescore winters, meet to-day.
One, only, is absent, — an unfortunate brother, bereft
of reason.

"But I must not dwell·upon reminiscences, be they sad or joyous; for our numerous friends who have honored us by their presence, despite the inclemency of the weather, have, for our Host and Hostess, words of congratulation. In our immediate family, no death has occurred for thirty-seven years; hence, come to-day five sons and two daughters, bringing their sheaves with them. Twenty grandchildren, buds of beauty, accompany us; and we twine them into a living wreath to-day, to crown the heads that yet stand erect under the weight of threescore and ten years.

"Again, I bid you a.cordial welcome to the joys and festivities of this pleasant occasion."

At the close of these remarks, a troop of grandchildren, of the eighth generation, came in, with a song of greeting; who, after giving and receiving each a kiss from their grandparents, dispersed among the older guests. A prayer of invocation was offered by Rev. S. Bush, pastor of the church in which the family has worshipped for many generations; after which, the company joined in singing the following hymn, to the grand old tune, "St. Martins:"—

> "Let children hear the mighty deeds
> Which God performed of old."

The company was then invited to listen to an address, prepared for the occasion by Rev. Dr. Allen, of Northboro', "the oldest living person born upon this spot, and the first among the Allens who received the honors of 'Old Harvard.'"

During the reading of the address, in which the doctor set forth so eloquently the remarkable traits of the ancestry on the father's side, it became evident that no notice was to be taken of the mother's pedigree; and as Joseph A., her third son, who is said to inherit many of her traits of character, was called upon, he responded in a happy sketch of her ancestry, tracing her descent, on both sides, directly from the "Mayflower;" and indulged in a humorous comparison of the merits of the Allens and Lanes. The pleasant repartee to which this gave rise, between the Rev. Doctor and the speaker, was the source of much amusement.

It was pleasant to see among the guests the venerable form of Colonel Obed Allen, — the oldest man present, nearly ninety years of age. Three of the guests of the wedding fifty years before were present; and also several of Mr. Allen's early schoolmates, — among them, Hon. Joseph Breek, of Brighton, whose benignant face seemed to show the sweet influence of the flowers which have been his companions for many years. In response to the call of the chairman, he made some pleasant allusions to the scenes of their early days.

Rev. Asa S. Allen, — who had journeyed fourteen hundred miles to celebrate this marriage-feast, — being called upon, responded in appropriate remarks.

Nathaniel T., the fourth son, here presented, with appropriate remarks, and read, letters of congratulation from William Lloyd Garrison, Wendell Phillips, Samuel J. May, Dr. Lowell Mason, Rev. Warren Burton, and others, who were unable to be present.

The following hymn, written for the occasion by one of the nephews, — T. Prentiss Allen, of New Bedford, — was read by him, and sung by the company : —

"Or ever the silver cord be loosed, or the golden bowl be broken."

O God! thy presence we entreat,
    As with our children here we come,
Each fond, familiar face to greet
    In this our dear ancestral home.

Before this family altar bowed,
    Our fathers raised their prayers to thee;
Here pledged their loyal faith, and vowed
    To live for truth and liberty.

For fifty years, thy servants here
    Have shared in love what thou hast given
Each gladdening joy, each bitter tear,
    Has brought them nearer thee and heaven.

For all these blessed years have brought;
    For children here or called above;
For mercies granted, lessons taught, —
    We give thee thanks, O God of Love!

So, when, upon this happy day,
    They pledge anew their love of old,
Bless them with thy rich grace, we pray,
    And in thy tender arms enfold.

And when is loosed the silver cord,
    And broke at last the golden bowl,
Grant them with thee, O gracious Lord!
    Th' eternal marriage of the soul.

The chairman then called upon James T., who, he said, though the youngest of the family, was considered old enough to speak for himself. He responded to the call, in a happy vein. A concluding prayer was then offered by Rev. Asa S. Allen, the brother from Wisconsin.

But before we left this feast of reason and true flow of soul, to partake of more substantial entertainment, it was whispered around that the impartial Muse had paid a visit to another guest; which, coming to the ear of the chairman, a demand was made upon Joseph Henry Allen, of Cambridge, another nephew, who gave this generous tribute to the family : —:

GOLDEN WEDDING, April 11, 1864.

Full fifty years have come and gone, their pleasure and their pain,
Since Ellis Allen carried home his young bride, Lucy Lane;
Their green spring then, their autumn now, so golden and serene,
And many a long, bright, sultry summer working-day, between.
Those years have laid their hand upon the bridegroom and the
    bride,
Frosty, but kindly; and, with days, their joys are multiplied.
Their children come to hear the words of plighted love again, —
Their daughters wedded matrons both, their sons five bearded men.
Their children's children gather too, and younger faces show
The joy and hope that entered here, just fifty years ago.
Some days were merry, some were sad, — their sunshine dashed
    with tears;
Yet dearer than the bride of youth, the wife of fifty years.

But, touch us ne'er so lightly, Time is sure to write his mark:
The merry village boy has grown a sober patriarch;
Gray hairs fringe scantily, where lay the locks of sunny brown;
The white beard gathers round the face, then smooth with boyish
    down;
The ruddy cheeks are furrowed with the lines of time and care;
The wide brow shows the histories that Life has written there.
But eye, lip, voice, and hand have kept the dear old mother-
    tongue,
True love is never out of date, the heart is always young!

Swiftly the generations pass : now, gathered here, we see
Seven goodly branches, bearing fruit, from this ancestral tree, —

New England's sons and daughters all, — once more together
    come,
To join this glad festivity, to greet this harvest-home.

The first, our model working-man, — a man of health and cheer;
Broad-chested, bearded, brown, — machinist, farmer, engineer.
A good and gentle name he bears, one ne'er dishonored yet,'—
Our William Cowper, with his wife, our loving Harriet.
His family of children, too, a long and fair array, —
Eight sturdy boys, two rosy girls, — salute us here to-day.

Then George, so strong and wise and good, so generous and kind,
We knew him in our boyish games, and still shall ever find.
He cannot have an enemy; and no one ever heard
One mean or cruel thing of him, one hard or angry word.
To something like a dozen boys, a father, true and mild;
And his and Susan's heart had room for one more orphan child.

A vaster family comes next; but never it annoys
The easy-tempered, cool, clear Head of some five hundred boys.
His tact and skill we know of old, — his music too, and fun;
Our Christmas sports must always wait for Joseph Addison.
Large-brained and shrewd, yet prompt and firm, quick-witted and
    alert:
Here are his girls, and here his frank, kind, cordial Lucy Burt.

Our Lucy next we greet, so dear, so womanly and true;
Now mistress of this pleasant home, — old home, but duties new.
We open all our hearts to her; we know her chequered life, —
The sorrows of the mother and the longing of the wife;
We weep that pure and noble heart, that young, proud, manly
    will:
Alas, our martyr-boy! alas, the field of Chancellorville!

Then Abby, dear, warm heart! between two good old Scripture
    names, —
The Apostle and the Israelite, — Nathaniel and James;
The cunning hand to organize, the genius that creates, —
No partners in a better work were ever better mates.

It needs no word of praise from us ; — the shrewdness, sense, and
    skill ;
The busy, patient, scheming brain ; the fixed and stubborn will ;
The tact and industry and thrift ; the system and the rule,
That wisely built and steadily maintain West-Newton school.

Forget we not to own, besides, the fortune that combines
With theirs the patient skill of our two sister Carolines ; ·
The wifely tact and tenderness, 'mid cares that still increase,
Which gives a home and mother's heart to twenty boys apiece !

The list above gives all except the daughters' husbands' names ; —
The Davises, — the citizen, and soldier ; Charles, and James.

We hail the day : while far away the war-clouds darkly lower,
We greet the sunshine of the Past ; we catch the golden hour.
We bless the kindly Providence that guards us still from harm ;
· God bless the noble old Bay State ! God bless the ALLEN FARM !

The family seemed to need no more : early friends
had gladdened the hour with pleasant reminiscences ;
brothers and cousins had poured out their offerings of
gratitude and love ; gray-haired men and venerable
women had given their presence, with hearts beating
responsive to the occasion ; and the pleasant odors of
old Java were inviting the attention to things which
cheer the inner man. Accordingly, the company was
divided into those over fifty, and those under that age.
The older ones were escorted to the dining-room, where
the generously spread table only waited for the bride to
place the knife in the beautiful loaf that graced its
centre, to dispense its bounties. An animated discus-
sion of these good things made the venerables willing
to give place to the younger party : and, by the time
they, in their turn, had done like justice to the enter-

tainment and themselves, the hour for departure had arrived; and, with warm congratulations, and fervent wishes for the future, — some with smiles, and some with tears, — the company departed.

Those who were left in the old home of seven generations gathered about its cheerful hearthstone, and recounted the pleasant sayings and doings, and all the circumstances which had conspired to make this the most memorable day of their lives, — a day the like of which may not shed its light upon either of the generations that participated in these festivities.

ADDRESS.

THE long-expected day has come; and, in the name of our hosts, and of those who have been instrumental in providing for this festive occasion, I bid you welcome to the old *hive*, which has sent out so many swarms to occupy other, and it may be richer, fields, to "gather honey from every opening flower."

By a happy coincidence, of which we were not apprised till a few days since, the Golden Wedding falls on the same month, and nearly on the same day, as the centennial of the birth of Phineas Allen, the father of the bridegroom, as also of the father-in-law of him who addresses you, Dr. H. Ware, Sr. ; the one having been born April 24, and the other April 1, 1764.

It will be understood, therefore, that we celebrate by this observance both events, — the wedding of the son, fifty years, and the birth of the father, a hundred years ago.

I propose, in this address, to give a sketch of the early history of the prolific family of the Allens of Medfield, which I hope will not be without interest to the connections, near and remote, whom the occasion

has brought together this day, and to other members of
the great family we represent.

The *paterfamilias,* — in Scripture phrase, "the
goodman of the house," — whose Golden Wedding we
are met to celebrate, is a lineal descendant, of the sixth
generation, of JAMES ALLEN, an emigrant from some
part of the island of Great Britain, probably of Scottish
descent, who became a freeman in the town of Dedham
in the year 1647.   Dedham at first embraced an extensive territory, forming, at the present time, the towns
of Medfield, Walpole, Wrentham, Dover, and Needham.   James Allen was one of the company of proprie-
tors to whom were assigned allotments of land in that
part of Dedham which, in 1650, was incorporated by
the name of "Medfield," or "Meadfield," in allusion to
the extensive meadows bordering on Charles River,
which forms the western boundary of the town.

I find, among the old papers which have been preserved in an oaken desk now in my possession, the following document, without date, but which appears to
have been the first grant of land now constituting the
old homestead.   The forms of the letters and the whole
appearance of the document indicate an early date : —

"Meadfield granteth to James Alin six Acres of Upland
that lieth on the north plaine, Abutting toward the west on
Stony Winter Brook, against the lands of Thomas Wight,
and on the waste lands on all other parts.

"HEN. ADAMS."

This six-acre lot probably included the site of the
house in which we are now assembled, and extended to

the small stream forming its western or rather south-western border, characteristically termed in the grant " Stony Winter Brook," as the ground through which it runs is literally paved with stones, and as the stream, though considerable in winter, almost disappears in summer. It is likely, however, that this, like most watercourses, was much larger before the forests were cleared away than we find it at the present time. It probably continued in a visible form till it reached " Home-Meadow Brook," so called, forming a well-defined boundary all the way through. The land on the other side of this small stream, now belonging to the homestead, was annexed long afterwards; the orchard purchased, of Colonel Johnson Mason, in the early part of this century, the pasture fifty or sixty years since.

We have no means of knowing what were the dimensions of the farm during the lifetime of James, the original proprietor. Undoubtedly, it was enlarged, from time to time, by additional grants and purchases, till it became a good-sized, though never a very large farm.

As there was " a cooper's-shop " standing in the time of King Philip's war, we conclude that our progenitor James Allen followed the humble but respectable occupation of a cooper, having learned the trade probably in the old country; in which profession he was followed by his youngest son, Joseph, and I believe his grandson Noah, who in succession inherited the home-place and the cooper's-shop. I do not know whether this shop was taken down, or removed to another place. Some of us remember well the old cellar where it stood, as I think we helped to fill it up with stones and earth.

We learn, from tradition in the family, that it was from this cooper's-shop that the Indians, under King Philip, in 1676, — on their way from Marlboro' to Medfield, which they laid in ashes, — took shavings, which they placed on the floor of the dwelling-house, setting it on fire, and then hurrying on to the village. Fortunately, the shavings were placed on a trap-door leading into the cellar; and the door having been consumed, and having fallen into the cellar, the fire was extinguished without farther harm.

It was a few years before this calamity, that Rev. John Allin, of Dedham, — a cousin of James, as we learn from a clause in his will, viz., Aug. 26, 1671, — died, "after an easy sickness of ten days," according to Cotton Mather, at the age of 75, having been born in 1596. "His beloved wife Katherine," as he calls her in his record, died three days after, and they were both buried in the same grave. She was his second wife, the widow of Governor Thomas Dudley, and was married to Rev. John Allin, Nov. 8, 1653, three months after the Governor's death, and a little more than six months after the death of Mr. A.'s first wife. They had three sons, — Benjamin, Daniel, and Eliezer; names preserved in other branches of the family.

Rev. John Allin and his wife Margaret came from Wrentham, County of Suffolk, England.

John, the oldest son of James Allen, was born in Dedham, Dec. 4, 1639, ten years before a settlement was made in that part of the town now Medfield. This settlement was "at a place nigh Bogastow," the Indian name of the interval on Charles River lying between Medfield on one side, and Medway and Sherborn on the other.

It has been, from time immemorial, a tradition in all branches of the family, that James and Anna Allen were emigrants from Scotland. There must have been some grounds for this universal belief. What has led me of late to doubt its correctness is that Rev. John Allin, the first minister of Dedham, — who, in his last will and testament, bequeathed a small legacy to his *cousin* James Allen, of Medfield, — came from England, and not Scotland ; and, besides, I am not aware that any emigrants from Scotland were among the first settlers of Massachusetts colony.

Still, it must be admitted that traditions like this have some foundation in fact ; and it is not unlikely, that, as I have already suggested, James or his wife, or both, were of Scottish extraction, and that they first went to England before embarking for this country. I shall be glad if we can find further evidence in confirmation of the tradition, which we have been accustomed to regard as quite satisfactory, — that the prolific family of the Allens of Medfield have the good old Covenanter blood running in their veins.

A brief account of the house and its surroundings, as they appeared in our boyhood at the beginning of this century, may not be uninteresting to the younger members of the family.

It was an old-fashioned, unpainted house of two stories, with a large chimney in the centre, the only ornament being a Doric scroll over the front door ; the

western part forming what is now the eastern part of
the building, including the front room and bedroom,
the door being in the centre, at what is now the south-
east corner of the house.   This part was occupied by
our grandparents Noah and Sybil Allen, his third wife.

The other part of the house stood nearer the road ;
at the south-east corner of which was the well, with its
curb and sweep and " moss-covered bucket ; " near which
stood the large horse-block, from the top of which we
mounted the old bay mare, father on the saddle, mother
on the pillion behind, and one of us boys, without saddle or pillion, riding before, astride the neck of the
patient and good-natured beast, that, without complaint,
bore her precious load to the village church, something
more than a mile distant.   To the north of the well and
horse-block, extending to the barn-yard, was a grass-
plot and garden, with peach-trees and a bed of fennel
near the road ; and farther west, partly occupied at the
present time by the kitchen and out-buildings, was the
kitchen-garden, with a square bed in the centre filled
with gay tulips and the gaudy peony, and other herbs
and flowers for use and ornament.

On part of the space between the kitchen-garden and
the road were several clumps of the pretty shrub, the
privet, so common in England, which with us went by
the name of " prim-bushes," and which were used as a
substitute for clothes-lines.

The barn stood on the same spot that it now occu-
pies, with its sloping yard in front, and stacks of
meadow-hay in the rear.

A few of us can remember the huge white-oak tree
which stood on the opposite side of the road, and with

what delight we children used to gather the ripened mast after a north-east storm in October, which we laid up for winter use, and which we thought almost as delicious as chestnuts. The trunk had been for many years a mere shell, when, during a violent gale, it fell, and great was the fall thereof; and great was our grief at the thought that it would yield no more its accustomed fruit.

I must not forget, nor pass by in silence, the old chestnut-tree, which stood, with its huge trunk and majestic arms, at the edge of the rock in the "Upper Orchard," as it was called, which was full six feet in diameter, and whose giant arms were stretched out over an area whose circumference could not have been much less than two hundred feet. We sometimes gathered from this single tree, on the morning following a severe storm of wind, from ten to fifteen quarts of its savory fruit.

We remember, too, — and the thought makes our mouths water, — we remember — oh, how could we forget? — the then long-lived peach-trees, laden every season with their luscious fruit, — three standing in a row in the Upper Orchard, and others near the house. Then the peach-tree knew neither the borer, nor that incurable disease the yellows. Then it flourished like other trees of the orchard, and seldom did it fail of yielding its fruit in its season.

A few other fruit-trees, coeval with the second generation at least, if not of the first, claim a moment's notice; and, among them, chief may be reckoned a gigantic pearmain, standing just below the cooper's-shop above mentioned, near the edge of the upland, which was our main dependence for winter fruit. The trunk was hollow as long ago as I can remember, and several persons — at least, several boys — could find shelter at the same time within its cavity. One of its huge arms stretched out towards the house, to the distance of thirty or forty feet, as if to claim kindred and fellowship with the departed occupants of the house, by whom it had been planted, — probably transplanted from the English home, — and who, in the days of its youthful vigor, had gathered its ripened fruit.

And there, below the barn-yard, stood the aged trunk, with a few scattered branches, — the old apple-tree, called, by way of distinction, — for its rich flavor and exceeding beauty, of a bright-red color, — " the Governor ; " and not far from it, and also in the orchard east of the house, flourished, in a green old age, some half-dozen specimens of the Seekonk sweeting, — a winter-apple excellent for baking, and which received its name, as we suppose, from Seekonk, R.I., from which place the patriarch Joseph, son of James, who inherited the old homestead, took his wife Hannah Sabine, and by whom he became the father of a numerous offspring.

And now let us follow the line of descent from our common progenitors James and Anna his wife, down to our friends who, in this old home and on this anniversary, renew the marriage-vows and solemn pledges mutually given and received just fifty years ago this day.

James Allen by Anna his wife, both emigrants from the Old World, had nine children ; viz., John, James, Nathaniel, William, Benjamin, Martha, Mary, Sarah, and Joseph.

The youngest of the sons was Joseph, born June 24, 1652, who, about 1675, married Hannah Sabine, of Seekonk, whose brother William had taken Joseph's sister Martha for his wife.

Joseph greatly enlarged, by purchase, the estate he inherited from his father, and appears to have been a man of energy and influence. As he increased in substance, so he was blessed with a numerous offspring, for whom he made provision as the sons arrived at man's estate, as also by his last will and testament, a copy of which is still preserved.

By this will, he made his son Noah the heir of the old homestead, and, among other legacies, bequeathed to his two sons Daniel and David a hundred acres of land, lying near Woodstock, Conn., and called by the Indian name " Massamoquit."

One of the sons, Nehemiah, settled, with some of the younger branches of the family, in Sturbridge; two others, Hezekiah and Eleazer, in Dover. One, Jeremiah, was killed by the Indians.

Numerous descendants of these three brothers may be found in those places, and others are scattered over different parts of the land.

Noah married Sarah Gay, of Dedham, by all accounts a woman of uncommon strength of character and capacity for business; qualities for which there was, in her case, special need, as her husband, for some years during the latter part of his life, was harmlessly but incurably insane. The care of the children and the management of the estate devolved upon her, and she showed herself equal to the task, ruling her household well, and directing her affairs with discretion.

She outlived her husband many years, and died in
1782, at the age of ninety; so that she was remembered
by many who were living half a century since, from
some of whom I learned the facts which I have just
narrated.

Noah died 1755, having just completed the term of
threescore years and ten.

The next in succession, of the fourth generation, of
those who lived on this spot, and inherited the estate,
was Noah Allen, Jr.; of whom some of us have a dis-
tinct and vivid recollection, as he died in 1804. He
was a tall, and in his prime a strong, athletic man;
of whom it is related, that, in a trial of strength, with
a horse for an antagonist, each competitor pulling at
the end of a common cart-rope, the rope snapped in
two, and neither party won the prize.

He was born in 1719, according to the record kept
by Rev. Joseph Baxter, the second minister of Medfield, and accordingly was eighty-five at the time of his
death.

Noah, by right of primogeniture, being the oldest
son, inherited a double portion of his father's estate; a
custom or law borrowed from England, and which continued in force till 1780.

Noah Allen, Jr., by his first wife, Miriam Fisher,
had five sons, — Asahel, Fisher, Silas, Gad, and
Nathan. Gad — whose Bible name, " a troop cometh,"
was given in reference to a troop of horsemen that
passed through the town at the time of his birth —
died in infancy.

Asahel died in early manhood, leaving three sons
and one daughter.

Of the other sons, Silas died at the age of eighty-four and six months; Fisher and Nathan, both at the age of ninety-five.

By his second wife, Abigail Ellis, he had one daughter, Miriam, — the kind-hearted, open-handed, whole-souled aunt, whose ample dimensions and sunny smiles and kindly greetings and motherly love are well remembered by the troops of nephews and nieces that were accustomed to visit her at her hospitable roof.

On April 24, 1764, the mother gave birth to a son, who received the Bible name, according to the custom of those days, of Phineas; the fifth in the order of succession that inherited the old homestead. The mother died the following summer (July 28), leaving her infant of three months to the care of others. Fortunately, the grandmother, Sarah [Gay] Allen, was still living, and by her watchful care supplied, as well as a grandmother could, the place of a mother to the infant child. The grandmother was spared to the great age of ninety years, at which time the motherless child was a young man of eighteen, a soldier in the continental army, in which he had enlisted at the early age of sixteen. He was at West Point at the time of Arnold's treason and the execution of the ill-fated Major André, and he shared in the privations and terrible sufferings that our army experienced in " the Jerseys." He returned at the close of the war, in a miserable plight, having marched the whole distance of two or three hundred miles on foot.

The other sons of Noah having been provided for, Phineas, the youngest of the family, married, and lived in the home-place, occupying the easterly end of the house, next to the street. Here all the children, excepting our youngest brother, first saw the light.

Our father married Oct. 22, 1787 (at the age of 23), Ruth, second daughter of Asa Smith, of Walpole, then only eighteen years old, to whose affectionate solicitude and untiring labors and watchful tender care we owe a debt of gratitude that we can never repay, and for which her children rise up and call her blessed.

We take a melancholy pleasure in recalling and recounting the pains taken by our honored parents to instil into our youthful minds good principles, — the love of truth, reverence for things sacred; to bring us up in habits of industry and sobriety; to encourage us in our desire to gain knowledge. We must not forget the sacrifices they made, the hardships they underwent, to gain the means for supporting three sons through a college course; the mother, especially, laboring beyond her strength, at unseasonable hours, and without much help except from the older children, — filling the place of mother and nurse, of seamstress and cook, and maid-of-all-work; often weary, but never disheartened; never thinking that she had done enough, while any duty remained unfulfilled.

Of the eight children, one, the first-born, — the sister who led me by the hand when first I was sent, a little child of four years, to the village-school, and whose sweet but somewhat grave countenance I can perfectly recall, — was taken from us at the age of seven, the victim of "the throat-distemper," as it was called; a disease which prevailed in the neighborhood, and proved fatal to many. The other children of the household, three in number, in turn took the disease; and one, our brother, for whom especially this anniversary is kept, barely escaped with his life.

As soon as the nature of the disease was known, we were all sent from home, and did not return till some time after the funeral; but I well remember how they brought us to the window, to look in upon the changed countenance of our sister and playmate, as laid out for burial. It was my first view of death, as it was the first great grief experienced by the bereaved parents; and the impressions it made were not soon effaced.

With this exception, all the children of Phineas and Ruth Allen have been spared to this day; and most of them, with the children whom God has given them, are present to join in this celebration. "Having obtained help of God, we continue to this time:" bearing marks of declining age indeed, but retaining a good share of health and vigor; and surrounded by blessings more than we can number, for which we owe our Maker and Preserver, our Heavenly Father and Friend, our fervent gratitude, our everlasting praises.

GOLDEN WEDDING OF GERSHOM AND ABIGAIL ADAMS.

GOLDEN WEDDING

GERSHOM AND ABIGAIL ADAMS.

T HE Golden Wedding of GERSHOM and ABIGAIL [ALLEN] ADAMS was celebrated at another of the old homesteads of Medfield, Nov. 12, 1868. The day was propitious, and a large company assembled, consisting of the children and grandchildren of the Bridegroom and Bride, and numerous relatives and friends, from places more or less remote, to whom invitations had been extended. Of the six brothers of Mrs. Adams, all but one were present; and only distance prevented the sixth (Rev. A. S. Allen, now living in Iowa) from joining the company. One of the sons, living in California, was necessarily absent. With this exception, all the descendants of the parties were gathered under the paternal roof, all rejoicing in health and prosperity. Alas! little did we think, that, within three short weeks, two of the guests, a nephew and a grandson (Rev. T. P. Allen and George Frederick Adams), would be called away, — the one at the noon, the other in the bright morning of life.*

---

* Rev. T. Prentiss Allen died Nov. 26, aged 46; George Frederick Adams died Dec. 6, aged 19.

After prayer by Rev. Mr. Bush (their former pastor), a number of letters from absent friends were read; among them, one in rhyme from Joseph A. Allen, of Fredonia, N.Y., filled with amusing reminiscences.

A hymn, written for the occasion by T. Prentiss Allen, was then sung; followed by an address from Rev. Dr. Allen, giving some history of the family of the Bridegroom, which had inhabited this spot for more than two hundred years.

A humorous description of the old homestead and the pleasant life there was next given, in verse, by Rev. J. H. Allen; a song, written for the occasion by George E. Allen, was sung by him with his brothers and sisters; and addresses from several friends present closed the exercises. Our friends received many valuable gifts; among which was a beautiful engraving of the "German Golden Wedding," presented by the neighbors and friends.

It was a delightful occasion, and long to be remembered by those who had the good fortune to be present, and share in the festivities.

HYMN, BY T. P. ALLEN.

Accept, O God! our grateful love, —
  The hallowed joy of this glad hour;
Thy peace brood o'er us as a dove,
  Thy Spirit move us by its power.

Blest day! — the light of fifty years, —
  When man and maid pledged faith and truth;
When wed, 'mid joy and sacred tears,
  The beauty and the strength of youth.

The bloom of beauty fadeth fast, —
   Man's youth and strength soon pass away:
Immortal love for aye will last,
   More pure and true from day to day.

The undoubting faith, that years increase;
   The hope and love, which ills control, —
These hallow life, and give sweet peace, —
   The Golden Marriage of the soul.

Thy children, Father, praises bring,
   For grief, for joy; for toil, for rest;
And more, — for glorious hopes that spring
   Eternal from the trustful breast.

When time for them shall be no more,
   And known no more the ways they trod,
Grant them, true wed, above to soar,
   And rest in thy dear arms, O God!

THE OLD HOUSE: AS HER NIECE MARY REMEMBERS IT.

TO MY AUNT, ON HER GOLDEN WEDDING.

I remember, I remember, — it is years and years ago, —
The old brown house; the meadows, where the river ran below;
The old elm-trees; the old gray barn; that old red horse the
   while,
Behind whose honest flanks I rode full many a dusty mile;
The old oak bucket in the well; the clear, cold draughts it drew;
Those sunny rooms, so snug and low, and hospitable too;
The quaint old kitchen, neat as wax; the bright old hickory blaze;
The old wide-throated chimney-place, that warmed those good old
   days;
The pots and kettles on the crane; the doughnuts simmering
   there,
While by the firelight sat " old Gran'ther Adams " in his chair;

The comfortable settle, and the chimney-corner seat,
Where George and Charley crowded in, all ruddy with the heat;
The great, uneven hearthstone, and the great old fire-dogs, —
Such huge hot fires I never saw, nor such great piles of logs!

I remember, I remember, on those pleasant winter days,
Before the sun above the hill could lift his earliest rays,
The breakfast done, the men at work, the boys all off at school,
The table cleared, the kitchen swept, I took my little stool, —
Then such a nice and cosey day, there by my dear aunt's side,
While songs she sang, and stories told, and busy fingers plied.
The day was never weary, from late sun to early shade;
And very proud was I to finish ten straw yards of braid!
The storm might beat, with wind and sleet, against the window-
    panes;
The snow might drift, all wild and swift, along the narrow lanes:
But, safe from storm, all bright and warm and merrily went the
    day;
And fast my winter visit passed, — too soon it passed away.

I remember, I remember, then, the glorious baking-days;
The great round oven, roaring hot; the pitchy pine-wood blaze, —
An oven big enough to hold five hundred loaves of bread! —
None of the little iron boxes now we see instead.
Fifteen great sticks we burnt to coal, then swept the coals all out;
Then earthen pots and baking-pans distributed about,
As thick as ever they could stand on that vast oven floor;
Well banked with embers glowing hot the heavy iron door,
That opened when the work was done; and there, all steaming, lay
The fragrant, hot, and wholesome spoils of that triumphant day : —
The great brown crusty loaves; the flaky mince and apple pies;
And custards, sweet and delicate, that met our hungry eyes.
Of all the dainties e'er I saw, those were the daintiest;
Of all good things, I always loved Aunt Abigail's the best, —
Unless it was Aunt Lucy's, — for I never quite could tell
Whose table I was fondest of, I loved them both so well!
And when, from one house to the other, either way I passed,
As nearly as I recollect I always chose the last!

I remember, I remember, too, my younger cousins three, —
John Quincy, years and years before he ever went to sea.

Poor fellow! by his mother's side he always had to stay,
Or else beside the kitchen fire to keep his cough away;
And learned all sorts of household skill, and culinary arts,
Which did him such good service when he lived in foreign parts.
Where is he now? Since I have heard, 'tis many a long year:
'Twould help bring back those good old days, if we could see him
    here.
And pale and serious cousin James, who grew to seventeen,
Then went, and left an aching void where his young life had been.
The weary, weary months and days he faded still, and pined, —
The fears that went before, and then the sorrow left behind.
And little cousin Robert, too, whom I remember well; —
How promising and beautiful I wish that I could tell;
How much was gathered up in him of hope and pride and joy;
How everybody knew and loved the darling little boy.
A bitter thing it is to see our youngest taken so:
One more bright star in heaven, but a lonelier life below.
But Time deals gently still, and dries the mother's tears that fall:
'Tis better to have loved and lost, than never love at all!

And Time has dealt with all of us since those old childish days:
Our tracks in life grow widening out; we walk our different ways;
Wall Street, or farm, camp, hospital, oil-wells or Turkish baths,
Ships, mines, and battle-fields bedeck our several chosen paths.
The group of cousins, once so near, in life are scattered wide,
As cares and gains and toils and pains with years are multiplied.
All the more precious to our hearts the love that changes not;
The pleasant memories that crown this hospitable spot;
The glad reminder of old times; the hope that ever cheers;
The comforts and the cares that wove these fifty golden years.

J. H. A

GOLDEN WEDDING.

BY G. E. ALLEN.

Tune, "BONNIE DOON."

Ye hills and plains of Medfield dear,
We come to meet you once again:
From homes afar, and homes more near,
We hail in love this Golden Twain.

We bring glad heart and joyous mind,
We leave our cares and toils behind,   ·
To celebrate this gladsome day,
And gifts upon its altar lay.

To few is given, through fifty years,
Such constant joy, so seldom tears;
A husband true, devoted, kind;
A spirit buoyant, pure, refined;

A voice in song and psalm so clear,
Melodious to our youthful ear, —
How oft we've run across the plain,
To hear anew that sweet refrain!

And now to Heaven our prayer we raise,
That health and strength and length of days,
The love of children, neighbor, friend,
Richly may bless you till the end.

Till then, dear Aunt, and Uncle too,
Accept our love, — 'tis warm and true;
And, while our devious way we're treading,
We'll ne'er forget this Golden Wedding.

THE END.

2197

ND - #0337 - 090123 - C0 - 229/152/5 - PB - 9781333871802 - Gloss Lamination